WHY READ?

Teacher: The One Who Made the Difference

*Nightmare on Main Street: Angels,
Sado-Masochism and the Culture of Gothic*

*Literature Against Philosophy, Plato to Derrida:
A Defence of Poetry*

*Wild Orchids and Trotsky:
Messages from American Universities (ed.)*

*Towards Reading Freud: Self-Creation in Milton,
Wordsworth, Emerson and Sigmund Freud*

WHY READ?

MARK EDMUNDSON

BLOOMSBURY

Published by Bloomsbury Publishing, New York and London
Distributed to the trade by Holtzbrinck Publishers

All papers used by Bloomsbury Publishing are natural, recyclable
products made from wood grown in well-managed
forests. The manufacturing processes conform to the
environmental regulations of the country of origin.

Library of Congress Cataloging-in-Publication Data

Edmundson, Mark, 1952–
Why read? / Mark Edmundson.—1st U.S. ed.
p. cm.
ISBN 1-58234-425-6
1. Literature—Study and teaching (Higher)—United States. 2. College students—
Books and reading—United States. 3. Education, Higher—United States.
4. Books and reading—United States. 1. Title.

PN70.E36 2004
807'.1'173—dc22
2004002401

First U.S. Edition 2004

1 3 5 7 9 10 8 6 4 2

Typeset by Hewer Text Ltd, Edinburgh
Printed in the United States of America
by Quebecor World Fairfield

For Matthew, Beloved Son

Books are the best of things, well used; abused, among the worst. What is the right use? What is the one end, which all means go to effect? They are for nothing but to inspire.

—Ralph Waldo Emerson, "The American Scholar"

Literary Life

READING THROUGH A volume of modern poetry not long ago, I came upon some lines that seemed to me to concentrate a strong and true sense of what there is to gain from great writing. The lines were by William Carlos Williams and they ran this way: "Look at / what passes for the new," Williams wrote. "You will not find it there but in / despised poems. / It is difficult / to get the news from poems / yet men die miserably every day / for lack / of what is found there." Williams asserts that though all of us are surrounded all the time with claims on our attention—film, TV, journalism, popular music, advertising, and the many other forms that pass for the new—there may be no medium that can help us learn to live our lives as well as poetry, and literature overall, can.

People die miserably every day for lack of what is found in despised poems—in literary artwork, in other words, that society at large denigrates. My own life and the lives of many others I've known offer testimony for what Williams has to say. Reading woke me up. It took me from a world of harsh limits into expanded possibility. Without poetry, without literature and art, I (and I believe many others, too) could well have died miserably. It was this belief in great writing that, thirty years ago, made me become a teacher.

Yet most of the people who do what I do now—who teach literature at colleges and universities—are far from believing Williams. Nearly all of them would find his lines overstated and idealizing. Many now see all of literature—or at least the kind of literature that's commonly termed canonical—as an outmoded form. It's been surpassed by theory, or rendered obsolete with the passage of time. To quote Williams on the value of poetry, without suitable condescension, at the next meeting of the Modern Language Association would be to invite no end of ridicule.

Does everyone who teaches literature hold this dismissive attitude? Not quite. But those who are better disposed to literary art tend to an extreme timidity. They find it embarrassing to talk about poetry as something that can redeem a life, or make it worth living. (Though they may feel these things to be true.) Those few professors who still hold literature in high regard often treat it aesthetically. Following Kant, they're prone to remove literary art from the push and toss of day-to-day life. They want to see poems and novels as autonomous artifacts that have earned the right to be disconnected from common experience. One admires great literary works as aesthetic achievements. But on actual experience, they should have no real bearing at all.

Other professors who still call themselves humanists are often so vague in their articulated sense of what great writing offers—it cultivates sensitivity; it augments imagination; it teaches tolerance—that their views are easily swept aside by the rigorous-sounding debunkers. Yet Williams is anything but vague. The most consequential poems offer something that is new—or, one might say "truth"—that makes significant life possible. Without such truth, one is in danger of miserable death, the kind of death that can come from living without meaning, without intensity, focus, or design.

The moral of this book is that Williams has it right. Poetry—literature in general—is *the* major cultural source of vital options for those who find that their lives fall short of their highest hopes. Literature is, I believe, our best goad toward new beginnings, our best chance for what we might call secular rebirth. However much society at large despises imaginative writing, however much those supposedly committed to preserve and spread literary art may demean it, the fact remains that in literature there abide major hopes for human renovation. This book is addressed to teachers. We teachers of literature, and of the humanities overall, now often stand between our students and their best aspirations, preventing them from getting what literary art has to offer. With all the resources at hand to help our students change their lives for the better, and despite real energy and dedication, most of us still fail in our most consequential task. Purportedly guides to greater regions of experience, we have become guards on the parapets, keeping others out.

This book is also written to students and potential students of literature—to all those who might dream of changing their current state through encounters with potent imaginations. You are invited to read over the shoulders of your teachers. You are invited, if need be, to supplant them: For much of what teachers can offer, you can provide for yourself. It is often simply a matter of knowing where to start. It's a matter of knowing what you might ask for and get from a literary education.

In Marcel Proust's *In Search of Lost Time*, there is a passage that gets close to the core of what a literary education should be about. The passage offers a deep sense of what we can ask from a consequential book. Proust speaks with the kind of clarity that is peculiarly his about what he hopes his work will achieve. In particular, he reflects on the relation he wants to strike with his readers. "It seemed to me," he observes, "that they would not be 'my' readers but readers of their own selves, my book being

merely a sort of magnifying glass like those which the optician at
Combray used to offer his customers—it would be my book but
with it I would furnish them the means of reading what lay inside
themselves. So that I would not ask them to praise me or to
censure me, but simply to tell me whether 'it really is like that.' I
should ask whether the words that they read within themselves
are the same as those which I have written."

What Proust is describing is an act of self-discovery on
the part of his reader. Immersing herself in Proust, the reader
may encounter aspects of herself that, while they have perhaps
been in existence for a long time, have remained unnamed,
undescribed, and therefore in a certain sense unknown. One
might say that the reader learns the language of herself; or
that she is humanly enhanced, enlarging the previously constricting circle that made up the border of what she's been. One
might also say, using another idiom, one that has largely
passed out of circulation, that her consciousness has been
expanded.

Proust's professed hope for his readers isn't unrelated to the
aims that Emerson, a writer Proust admired, attributes to the
ideal student he describes in "The American Scholar": "One
must be an inventor to read well. As the proverb says, 'He that
would bring home the wealth of the Indies, must carry out the
wealth of the Indies.' There is then creative reading as well as
creative writing. When the mind is braced by labor and invention, the page of whatever book we read becomes luminous with
manifold allusion. Every sentence is doubly significant, and the
sense of our author is as broad as the world."

For Emerson, the reader can do more than discover the
language of herself in great writing. Emerson's reader uses a
book as an imaginative goad. He can begin compounding
visions of experience that pass beyond what's manifest in the

book at hand. This, presumably, is what happened when Shakespeare read Holinshed's *Chronicles* or even Plutarch's *Lives*. These are major sources for the plays, yes, but in reading them Shakespeare made their sentences doubly significant, and the sense of their authors as broad as the world.

Proust and Emerson touch on two related activities that are central to a true education in the humanities. The first is the activity of discovering oneself as one is in great writing. The second, and perhaps more important, is to see glimpses of a self—and too, perhaps, of a world—that might be, a self and world that you can begin working to create. "Reading," Proust says in a circumspect mood, "is on the threshold of the spiritual life; it can introduce us to it; it does not constitute it."

Proust and Emerson point toward a span of questions that matter especially for the young, though they count for us all, too. They are questions that should lie at the core of a liberal arts education. Who am I? What might I become? What is this world in which I find myself? How might it be changed for the better?

We ought to value great writing preeminently because it enjoins us to ask and helps us to answer these questions, and others like them. It helps us to create and re-create ourselves, often against harsh odds. So I will be talking here about the crafting of souls, in something of the spirit that Socrates did. "This discussion," Socrates said, referring to one of his philosophical exchanges, "is not about any chance question, but about the way one should live."

I think that the purpose of a liberal arts education is to give people an enhanced opportunity to decide how they should live their lives. So I will be talking about the uses of the liberal arts for the conduct of life. I will be describing the humanities as a source of truth. I will be asking teachers to think back to the days when reading and thinking about books first swept them in and changed them, and asking them to help their students have that kind of transforming experience.

A reader removed from the debates about the liberal arts that have been going on over the past few decades would, on hearing the aims for this book, perhaps smile at how superfluous and unoriginal they seem. Of course, universities should present humanities students with what Matthew Arnold called "the best that is known and thought" and give them the chance to reaffirm or remake themselves based on what they find.

To the charge of lacking originality, I plead guilty. I have already cited Proust and Emerson; this book will be filled with the wisdom of many others, often similarly well-known. But as to my argument being superfluous: I can assure you that is not the case. Universities now are far from offering the kind of experience that Allan Bloom, a writer with whose work I have something like a love-hate relationship, is describing when he observes that "true liberal education requires that the student's whole life be radically changed by it, that what he learns may affect his action, his tastes, his choices, that no previous attachment be immune to examination and hence re-evaluation. Liberal education puts everything at risk and requires students who are able to risk everything."

By this definition, true liberal education barely exists in America now. It is almost nowhere to be found. We teachers have become timid and apologetic. We are not willing to ask the questions that matter. Into the void that we have created largely by our fear, other forces have moved. Universities have become sites not for human transformation, but for training and for entertaining. Unconfronted by major issues, students use the humanities as they can. They use them to prepare for lucrative careers. They acquire marketable skills. Or, they find in their classes sources of easy pleasure. They read to enjoy, but not to become other than they are. "You must change your life," says Rilke's sculpture of Apollo to the beholder. So says every major work of intellect and imagination, but in the university now—as in the culture at large—almost no one hears.

Total Entertainment All the Time

I CAN DATE my sense that something was going badly wrong in my own teaching to a particular event. It took place on evaluation day in a class I was giving on the works of Sigmund Freud. The class met twice a week, late in the afternoon, and the students, about fifty undergraduates, tended to drag in and slump, looking slightly disconsolate, waiting for a jump start. To get the discussion moving, I often provided a joke, an anecdote, an amusing query. When you were a child, I had asked a few weeks before, were your Halloween costumes id costumes, superego costumes, or ego costumes? Were you monsters—creatures from the black lagoon, vampires, and werewolves? Were you Wonder Women and Supermen? Or were you something in between? It often took this sort of thing to raise them from the habitual torpor.

But today, evaluation day, they were full of life. As I passed out the assessment forms, a buzz rose up in the room. Today they were writing their course evaluations; their evaluations of Freud, their evaluations of me. They were pitched into high gear. As I hurried from the room, I looked over my shoulder to see them scribbling away like the devil's auditors. They were writing furiously, even the ones who struggled to squeeze out their papers and journal entries word by word.

But why was I distressed, bolting out the door of my classroom, where I usually held easy sway? Chances were that the evaluations would be much like what they had been in the past: they'd be just fine. And in fact, they were. I was commended for being "interesting," and complimented for my relaxed and tolerant ways; my sense of humor and capacity to connect the material we were studying with contemporary culture came in for praise.

In many ways, I was grateful for the evaluations, as I always had been, just as I'm grateful for the chance to teach in an excellent university surrounded everywhere with very bright people. But as I ran from that classroom, full of anxious intimations, and then later as I sat to read the reports, I began to feel that there was something wrong. There was an undercurrent to the whole process I didn't like. I was disturbed by the evaluation forms themselves with their number ratings ("What is your ranking of the instructor?—1, 2, 3, 4, or 5"), which called to mind the sheets they circulate after a TV pilot plays to the test audience in Burbank. Nor did I like the image of myself that emerged—a figure of learned but humorous detachment, laid-back, easygoing, cool. But most of all, I was disturbed by the attitude of calm consumer expertise that pervaded the responses. I was put off by the serenely implicit belief that the function of Freud—or, as I'd seen it expressed on other forms, in other classes, the function of Shakespeare, of Wordsworth or of Blake—was diversion and entertainment. "Edmundson has done a fantastic job," said one reviewer, "of presenting this difficult, important & controversial material in an enjoyable and approachable way."

Enjoyable: I enjoyed the teacher. I enjoyed the reading. Enjoyed the course. It was pleasurable, diverting, part of the culture of readily accessible, manufactured bliss: the culture of Total Entertainment All the Time.

As I read the reviews, I thought of a story I'd heard about a Columbia University instructor who issued a two-part question at the end of his literature course. Part one: What book in the course did you most dislike? Part two: What flaws of intellect or character does that dislike point up in you? The hand that framed those questions may have been slightly heavy. But at least they compelled the students to see intellectual work as a confrontation between two people, reader and author, where the stakes mattered. The Columbia students were asked to relate the quality of an encounter, not rate the action as though it had unfolded across the big screen. A form of media connoisseurship was what my students took as their natural right.

But why exactly were they describing the Oedipus complex and the death drive as interesting and enjoyable to contemplate? Why were they staring into the abyss, as Lionel Trilling once described his own students as having done, and commending it for being a singularly dark and fascinatingly contoured abyss, one sure to survive as an object of edifying contemplation for years to come? Why is the great confrontation—the rugged battle of fate where strength is born, to recall Emerson—so conspicuously missing? Why hadn't anyone been changed by my course?

To that question, I began to compound an answer. We Americans live in a consumer culture, and it does not stop short at the university's walls. University culture, like American culture at large, is ever more devoted to consumption and entertainment, to the using and using up of goods and images. We Americans are six percent of the world's population: we use a quarter of its oil; we gorge while others go hungry; we consume everything with a vengeance and then we produce movies and TV shows and ads to celebrate the whole consumer loop. We make it—or we appropriate it—we "enjoy" it and we burn it up, pretty much whatever "it" is. Someone coming of age in America now, I thought, has few available alternatives to the consumer world-view. Students didn't ask for it, much less create it, but they brought a consumer Weltanschauung to school, where it exerted a potent influence.

The students who enter my classes on day one are generally devotees of spectatorship and of consumer-cool. Whether they're sorority-fraternity denizens, piercer-tattooers, gay or straight, black or white, they are, nearly across the board, very, very self-contained. On good days, there's a light, appealing glow; on bad days, shuffling disgruntlement. But there is little fire, little force of spirit or mind in evidence.

More and more, we Americans like to watch (and not to do). In fact watching is our ultimate addiction. My students were the progeny of two hundred available cable channels and omnipresent Blockbuster outlets. They grew up with their noses pressed against the window of that second spectral world that spins parallel to our own, the World Wide Web. There they met life at second or third hand, peering eagerly, taking in the passing show, but staying remote, apparently untouched by it. So conditioned, they found it almost natural to come at the rest of life with a sense of aristocratic expectation: "What have you to show me that I haven't yet seen?"

But with this remove comes timidity, a fear of being directly confronted. There's an anxiety at having to face life firsthand. (The way the word "like" punctuates students' speech—"I was like really late for like class"—indicates a discomfort with immediate experience and a wish to maintain distance, to live in a simulation.) These students were, I thought, inclined to be both lordly and afraid.

The classroom atmosphere they most treasured was relaxed, laid-back, cool. The teacher should never get exercised about anything, on pain of being written off as a buffoon. Nor should she create an atmosphere of vital contention, where students lost their composure, spoke out, became passionate, expressed their deeper thoughts and fears, or did anything that might cause embarrassment. Embarrassment was the worst thing that could befall one; it must be avoided at whatever cost.

Early on, I had been a reader of Marshall McLuhan, and I was reminded of his hypothesis that the media on which we as a culture have become dependent are themselves cool. TV, which seemed on the point of demise, so absurd had it become to the culture of the late sixties, rules again. To disdain TV now is bad form; it signifies that you take yourself far too seriously. TV is a tranquilizing medium, a soporific, inducing in its devotees a light narcosis. It reduces anxiety, steadies and quiets the nerves. But it also deadens. Like every narcotic, it will, consumed in certain doses, produce something like a hangover, the habitual watchers' irritable languor that persists after the TV is off. It's been said that the illusion of knowing and control that heroin engenders isn't entirely unlike the TV consumer's habitual smug-torpor, and that seems about right.

Those who appeal most on TV over the long haul are low-key and nonassertive. Enthusiasm quickly looks absurd. The form of character that's most ingratiating on the tube, that's most in tune with the medium itself, is laid-back, tranquil, self-contained, and self-assured. The news anchor, the talk-show host, the announcer, the late-night favorite—all are prone to display a sure sense of human nature, avoidance of illusion, reliance on timing and strategy rather than on aggressiveness or inspiration. With such figures, the viewer is invited to identify. On what's called reality TV, on game shows, quiz shows, inane contests, we see people behaving absurdly, outraging the cool medium with their firework personalities. Against such excess the audience defines itself as worldly, laid-back, and wise.

Is there also a financial side to the culture of cool? I believed that I saw as much. A cool youth culture is a marketing bonanza for producers of the right products, who do all they can to enlarge that culture and keep it humming. The Internet, TV, and magazines teem with what I came to think of as persona ads, ads for Nikes and Reeboks and Jeeps and Blazers that don't so much endorse the powers of the product per se as show you what sort of person you'll inevitably become once you've acquired it. The Jeep ad that featured hip outdoorsy kids flinging a Frisbee from mountaintop to mountaintop wasn't so much about what Jeeps can do as it was about the kind of people who own them: vast, beautiful creatures, with godlike prowess and childlike tastes. Buy a Jeep and be one with them. The ad by itself is of little consequence, but expand its message exponentially and you have the central thrust of postmillennial consumer culture: buy in order to be. Watch (coolly) so as to learn how to be worthy of being watched (while being cool).

To the young, I thought, immersion in consumer culture, immersion in cool, is simply felt as natural. They have never known a world other than the one that accosts them from every side with images of mass-marketed perfection. Ads are everywhere: on TV, on the Internet, on billboards, in magazines, sometimes plastered on the side of the school bus. The forces that could challenge the consumer style are banished to the peripheries of culture. Rare is the student who arrives at college knowing something about the legacy of Marx or Marcuse, Gandhi or Thoreau. And by the time she does encounter them, they're presented as diverting, interesting, entertaining—or perhaps as objects for rigorously dismissive analysis—surely not as guides to another kind of life.

As I saw it, the specter of the uncool was creating a subtle tyranny for my students. It's apparently an easy standard to subscribe to, the standard of cool, but once committed to it, you discover that matters are different. You're inhibited, except on ordained occasions, from showing feeling, stifled from trying to achieve anything original. Apparent expressions of exuberance now seem to occur with dimming quotation marks around them. Kids celebrating at a football game ironically play the roles of kids celebrating at a football game, as it's been scripted on multiple TV shows and ads. There's always self-observation, no real letting-go. Students apparently feel that even the slightest departure from the reigning code can get you genially ostracized. This is a culture tensely committed to a laid-back norm.

In the current university environment, I saw, there was only one form of knowledge that was generally acceptable. And that was knowledge that allowed you to keep your cool. It was fine to major in economics or political science or commerce, for there you could acquire ways of knowing that didn't compel you to reveal and risk yourself. There you could stay detached. And—what was at least as important—you could acquire skills that would stand you in good financial stead later in life. You could use your education to make yourself rich. All of the disciplines that did not traduce the canons of cool were thriving. It sometimes seemed that every one of my first-year advisees wanted to major in economics, even when they had no independent interest in the subject. They'd never read an economics book, had no attraction to the business pages of the *Times*. They wanted economics because word had it that econ was the major that made you look best to Wall Street and the investment banks. "We like economics majors," an investment banking recruiter reportedly said, "because they're people who're willing to sacrifice their educations to the interest of their careers."

The subjects that might threaten consumer cool, literary study in particular, had to adapt. They could offer diversion—it seems that's what I (and Freud) had been doing—or they could make themselves over to look more like the so-called hard, empirically based disciplines.

Here computers come in. Now that computers are everywhere, each area of enquiry in the humanities is more and more defined by the computer's resources. Computers are splendid research tools. Good. The curriculum turns in the direction of research. Professors don't ask students to try to write as Dickens would, experiment with thinking as he might, were he alive today. Rather, they research Dickens. They delve into his historical context; they learn what the newspapers were gossiping about on the day that the first installment of *Bleak House* hit the stands. We shape our tools, McLuhan said, and thereafter our tools shape us.

Many educated people in America seem persuaded that the computer is the most significant invention in human history. Those who do not master its intricacies are destined for a life of shame, poverty, and neglect. Thus more humanities courses are becoming computer-oriented, which keeps them safely in the realm of cool, financially negotiable endeavors. A professor teaching Blake's "The Chimney Sweeper," which depicts the exploitation of young boys whose lot is not altogether unlike the lot of many children living now in American inner cities, is likely to charge his students with using the computer to compile as much information about the poem as possible. They can find articles about chimney sweepers from 1790s newspapers; contemporary pictures and engravings that depict these unfortunate little creatures; critical articles that interpret the poem in a seemingly endless variety of ways; biographical information on Blake, with hints about events in his own boyhood that would have made chimney sweepers a special interest; portraits of the author at various stages of his life; maps of Blake's London. Together the class might create a Blake–Chimney Sweeper website: *www.blakesweeper.edu*. Instead of spending class time wondering what the poem means, and what application it has to present-day experience, students compile information about it. They set the poem in its historical and critical context, showing first how the poem is the product and the property of the past—and, implicitly, how it really has nothing to do with the present except as an artful curiosity—and second how, given the number of ideas about it already available, adding more thoughts would be superfluous.

By putting a world of facts at the end of a key-stroke, computers have made facts, their command, their manipulation, their ordering, central to what now can qualify as humanistic education. The result is to suspend reflection about the differences among wisdom, knowledge, and information. Everything that can be accessed online can seem equal to everything else, no datum more important or more profound than any other. Thus the possibility presents itself that there really is no more wisdom; there is no more knowledge; there is only information. No thought is a challenge or an affront to what one currently believes.

Am I wrong to think that the kind of education on offer in the humanities now is in some measure an education for empire? The people who administer an empire need certain very precise capacities. They need to be adept technocrats. They need the kind of training that will allow them to take up an abstract and unfelt relation to the world and its peoples—a cool relation, as it were. Otherwise, they won't be able to squeeze forth the world's wealth without suffering debilitating pains of conscience. And the denizen of the empire needs to be able to consume the kinds of pleasures that will augment his feeling of rightful rulership. Those pleasures must be self-inflating and not challenging; they need to confirm the current empowered state of the self and not challenge it. The easy pleasures of this nascent American empire, akin to the pleasures to be had in first-century Rome, reaffirm the right to mastery—and, correspondingly, the existence of a world teeming with potential vassals and exploitable wealth.

Immersed in preprofessionalism, swimming in entertainment, my students have been sealed off from the chance to call everything they've valued into question, to look at new ways of life, and to risk everything. For them, education is knowing and lordly spectatorship, never the Socratic dialogue about how one ought to live one's life.

These thoughts of mine didn't come with any anger at my students. For who was to blame them? They didn't create the consumer biosphere whose air was now their purest oxygen. They weren't the ones who should have pulled the plug on the TV or disabled the game port when they were kids. They hadn't invited the ad flaks and money changers into their public schools. What I felt was an ongoing sense of sorrow about their foreclosed possibilities. They seemed to lack chances that I, born far poorer than most of them, but into a different world, had abundantly enjoyed.

As I read those evaluation forms and thought them over, I recalled a story. In Vienna, there was once a superb teacher of music, very old. He accepted few students. There came to him once a young man whom all of Berlin was celebrating. Only fourteen, yet he played exquisitely. The young man arrived in Austria hoping to study with the master. At the audition, he played to perfection; everyone surrounding the old teacher attested to the fact. When it came time to make his decision, the old man didn't hesitate. "I don't want him," he said. "But, master, why not?" asked a protégé. "He's the most gifted young violinist we've ever heard." "Maybe," said the old man. "But he lacks something, and without this thing real development is not possible. What that young man lacks is inexperience." It's a precious possession, inexperience; my students have had it stolen from them.

Cool School

BUT WHAT ABOUT the universities themselves? Do they do all they can to fight the reign of consumer cool?

From the start, the university's approach to students now has a solicitous, maybe even a servile tone. As soon as they enter their junior year in high school, and especially if they live in a prosperous zip code, the information materials, which is to say the advertising, come rolling in. Pictures, testimonials, videocassettes and CD-ROMs (some bidden, some not) arrive at the door from colleges across the country, all trying to capture the students and their tuition dollars.

The freshman-to-be sees photographs of well-appointed dorm rooms; of elaborate phys-ed facilities; of expertly maintained sports fields; of orchestras and drama troupes; of students working joyously, off by themselves. It's a retirement spread for the young. "Colleges don't have admissions offices anymore, they have marketing departments," a school financial officer said to me once. Is it surprising that someone who has been approached with photos and tapes, bells and whistles, might come to college thinking that the Shakespeare and Freud courses were also going to be agreeable treats?

How did we reach this point? In part, the answer is a matter of demographics and also of money. Aided by the GI Bill, the college-going population increased dramatically after the Second World War. Then came the baby boomers, and to accommodate them colleges continued to grow. Universities expand readily enough, but with tenure locking in faculty for lifetime jobs, and with the general reluctance of administrators to eliminate their own slots, it's not easy for a university to contract. So after the baby boomers had passed through—like a tasty lump sliding the length of a boa constrictor—the colleges turned to promotional strategies—to advertising—to fill the empty chairs. Suddenly college, except for the few highly selective establishments, became a buyers' market. What students and their parents wanted had to be taken potently into account. That often meant creating more comfortable, less challenging environments, places where almost no one failed, everything was enjoyable, and everyone was nice.

Just as universities must compete with one another for students, so must individual departments. At a time of rank economic anxiety (and what time is not in America?), the English department and the history department have to contend for students against the more success-ensuring branches, such as the science departments and the commerce school. In 1968, more than 21 percent of all the bachelor's degrees conferred in America were humanities degrees; by 1993 that total had fallen to about 13 percent, and it continues to sink. The humanities now must struggle to attract students, many of whose parents devoutly wish that they would go elsewhere.

One of the ways we've tried to be attractive is by loosening up.

We grade much more genially than our colleagues in the sciences. In English and history, we don't give many D's, or C's, either. (The rigors of Chem 101 may create almost as many humanities majors per year as the splendors of Shakespeare.) A professor at Stanford explained that grades were getting better because the students were getting smarter every year. Anything, I suppose, is possible.

Along with easing up on grades, many humanities departments have relaxed major requirements. There are some good reasons for introducing more choice into the curricula and requiring fewer standard courses. But the move jibes with a tendency to serve the students instead of challenging them. Students can float in and out of classes during the first two weeks of the term without making any commitment. The common name for this span—shopping period—attests to the mentality that's in play.

One result of the university's widening elective leeway is to give students more power over teachers. Those who don't like you can simply avoid you. If the students dislike you en masse, you can be left with an empty classroom. I've seen other professors, especially older ones, often those with the most to teach, suffer real grief at not having enough students sign up for their courses: their grading was too tough; they demanded too much; their beliefs were too far out of line with the existing dispensation. It takes only a few such incidents to draw other professors into line.

Before students arrive, universities ply them with luscious ads, guaranteeing them a cross between summer camp and lotusland. When they get to campus, flattery, entertainment, and preprofessional training are theirs, if that's what they want. The world we present them is not a world elsewhere, an ivory tower world, but one that's fully continuous with the American entertainment and consumer culture they've been living in. They hardly know they've left home. Is it a surprise, then, that this generation of students—steeped in consumer culture before they go off to school; treated as potent customers by the university well before they arrive, then pandered to from day one—are inclined to see the books they read as a string of entertainments to be enjoyed without effort or languidly cast aside?

So I had my answer. The university had merged almost seamlessly with the consumer culture that exists beyond its gates. Universities were running like businesses, and very effective businesses at that. Now I knew why my students were greeting great works of mind and heart as consumer goods. They came looking for what they'd had in the past, Total Entertainment All the Time, and the university at large did all it could to maintain the flow. (Though where this allegiance to the Entertainment-Consumer Complex itself came from—that is a much larger question. It would take us into politics and economics, becoming, in time, a treatise in itself.)

But what about me? Now I had to look at my own place in the culture of training and entertainment. Those course evaluations made it clear enough. I was providing diversion. To some students I was offering an intellectualized midday variant of Letterman and Leno. They got good times from my classes, and maybe a few negotiable skills, because that's what I was offering. But what was I going to do about it? I had diagnosed the problem, all right, but as yet I had nothing approaching a plan for action.

I'd like to say that I arrived at something like a breakthrough simply by delving into my own past. In my life I've had a string of marvelous teachers, and thinking back on them was surely a help. But some minds—mine, at times, I confess—tend to function best in opposition. So it was looking not just to the great and good whom I've known, but to something like an arch-antagonist, that got me thinking in fresh ways about how to teach and why.

The World According to Falwell

I TEACH AT the University of Virginia, and not far from me, down Route 29 in Lynchburg—whence the practice of lynching, some claim, gets its name—is the church of Jerry Falwell. Falwell teaches "the word of God," the literal, unarguable truth as it's revealed to him in the Bible and as it must be understood by all heaven-bound Christians.

For some time, I thought that we at the University of Virginia had nothing consequential to do with the Reverend Falwell. Occasionally, I'd get a book through interlibrary loan from Falwell's Liberty University; sometimes the inside cover contained a warning to the pious suggesting that though this volume might be the property of the Liberty University library, its contents, insofar as they contradict the Bible (which means the Bible according to Falwell) were of no particular value.

It's said that when a certain caliph was on the verge of burning the great library at Alexandria, scholars fell on their knees in front of him and begged him to relent. "There are two kinds of books here," the caliph purportedly said. "There are those that contradict the Koran—they are blasphemous. There are those that corroborate the Koran—they are superfluous." So: "Burn the library." Given the possibilities for fundamentalist literary criticism that the caliph opened up, it's a good thing that Liberty has a library at all.

Thomas Jefferson, the University of Virginia's founder, was a

deist, maybe something more scandalous than that, the ortho-
dox of Virginia used to whisper. The architecture of my university's central grounds, all designed by Jefferson, is
emphatically secular, based on Greek and Roman models. In
fact, the Rotunda, once the university's library, is designed in
homage to the Roman Pantheon, a temple to the twelve chief
pagan gods. Where the statues of those gods stand in the
Pantheon, there, in the Rotunda library, were books. Books
were Jefferson's deities, invested with powers of transport and
transformation equal to anything the ancient gods possessed. As
soon as they saw the new university, local divines went apo-
plectic. Where was the church? Unlike Princeton and Harvard,
the state university didn't have a Christian house of worship at
its center. From pulpits all over Virginia, ministers threatened
the pagan enclave with ruin from above. In 1829, the Episcopal
bishop William Meade predicted the university's ruin, because,
as he put it, the "Almighty is angry" about the Rotunda. (It's
probably only fair to report that in 1895 the Rotunda did burn
down.)

Jefferson—deist (maybe worse), scientist, cosmopolitan—
seems to have believed that the best way to deal with religion
was to banish it, formally, from the university, and instead to
teach the useful arts of medicine, commerce, law, and the rest.
The design of my university declares victory over what the
radicals of the Enlightenment would have called superstition,
and what most Americans currently call faith or spirituality. And
we honor Jefferson now by, in effect, rendering unto Falwell that
which is Falwell's.

In fact, we—and I don't mean only at the University of
Virginia; I mean humanists in general—have entered into an
implied bargain with Falwell and other American promulgators
of faith, most of whom have much more to recommend them

than the Prophet of Lynchburg. They do the soul-crafting. They administer the spiritual education. They address the hearts of our students, and in some measure of the nation at large. We preside over the minds. We shape intelligences; we train the faculties (and throw in more than a little entertainment on the side). In other words, we teachers strike an unspoken agreement with religion and its dispensers. They do their work, we do ours.

But isn't that the way it should be? Isn't religion private? Spirituality, after all, is everyone's personal affair; it shouldn't be the substance of college education; it should be passed over in silence. What professor would have the bad taste to puncture the walls of his students' privacy, to invade their inner lives, by asking them uncomfortable questions about ultimate values?

Well, it turned out, me. I decided that I was, in a certain sense, going to take my cue from religion. After all, I got into teaching for the same reason, I suspect, that many people did: because I thought it was a high-stakes affair, a pursuit in which souls are won and lost.

"How do you imagine God?" If you are going to indulge in embarrassing behavior, if you're going to make your students "uncomfortable," why not go all the way? This question has moved to the center of many of my classes—not classes in religion, but classes in Shakespeare, in Romantic poetry, in major nineteenth-century novels. That is, the embarrassing question begins courses with which, according to Jefferson, according to Falwell and other, more tempered advocates of faith, and according to the great majority of my colleagues in the humanities, it has absolutely nothing to do.

What kind of answers do I get? Often marvelous ones. After

the students who are disposed to walk out have, sometimes leaving an editorial sigh hanging in the air, and after there's been a weekend for reflection, answers come forth. Some of the accounts are on the fluffy side. I've learned that God is love and only love; I've heard that God is Nature; that God is light; that God is all the goodness in the universe. I hear tales about God's interventions into the lives of my students, interventions that save them from accidents, deliver them from sickness while others fall by the wayside. There's a whole set of accounts that are on the all-benevolent side—smiling, kindly, but also underramified, insufficiently thought-out. If God is all things, or abides in all things, then what is the source of evil? (By now, it's clear to the students that bad taste is my game; already I'm getting a little by way of indulgence.) A pause, then an answer, sometimes not a bad one. The most memorable exponent of smiling faith was a woman named Catherine, who called her blend of creamy benevolence—what else?—Catherinism.

But I respected Catherine for speaking as she did, for unfolding herself bravely. In general, humanities classes, where questions of ultimate belief should be asked and answered all the time, have nothing to do with those questions. It takes courage to make this first step, and to speak candidly about yourself.

Some of the responses are anything but underelaborated. These tend to come from my orthodoxly religious students, many of whom are well trained, maybe overtrained, in the finer points of doctrine. I get some hardcore believers. But in general it wouldn't be fair to call them Falwell's children, because they're often among the most thoughtful students in the class. They, unlike the proponents of the idea that God is light and that's all you need to know in life, are interested in delving into major questions. They care about understanding the source of evil. They want to know what it means to live a good life. And though they're rammed with doctrine, they're not always addicted to dogma. There's often more than a little room for doubt. Even if their views are sometimes rock solid, they don't mind seeing them besieged. Because given their interests, they're glad that "this discussion is not about any chance question, but about the way one should live."

Final Narratives

RELIGION IS THE right place to start a humanities course, for a number of reasons, even if what we're going on to do is to read the novels of Henry James. One of them is that religion is likely to be a major element in my students' Final Narratives, a term I adapt from Richard Rorty. A Final Narrative (Rorty actually says Final Vocabulary; I modify him slightly) involves the ultimate set of terms that we use to confer value on experience. It's where our principles are manifest. When someone talks feelingly about the Ten Commandments, or the Buddha's Four Noble Truths, or the innate goodness of human beings, or about all human history being the history of class conflict, then, in all likelihood, she has revealed something close to the core of her being. She's touched on her ultimate terms of commitment, the point beyond which argument and analysis are unlikely to go, at least very quickly. Rorty puts it this way: "All human beings carry about a set of words which they employ to justify their actions, their beliefs, and their lives. These are the words in which we formulate praise of our friends and contempt for our enemies, our long-term projects, our deepest self-doubts and our highest hopes. They are the words

in which we tell, sometimes prospectively and sometimes retro-
spectively, the story of our lives."

Rorty's word "final" is ironic, or potentially so. His sense is
that a "final" language ought to be anything but final. He
believes that we ought to be constantly challenging, testing,
refining, and if need be overthrowing our ultimate terms and
stories, replacing them with others that serve us better. Certain
people, says Rorty, are "always aware that the terms in which
they describe themselves are subject to change, always aware of
the contingency and fragility of their final vocabularies, and thus
of their selves." But Rorty believes that most people never stray
far from their initial narratives, the values that they're imprinted
with while they're growing up. Most of us stay at home.

Rorty calls people capable of adopting new languages "ironists," because they inflect even their most fervent commitments with doubt. It's possible, they know, that what today
they hold most intimately true will be replaced tomorrow by
other, better ways of seeing and saying things. They compre-
hend what Rorty likes to call the contingency of their own
current state.

Appreciating this contingency is very close to appreciating
one's own mortality. That is, Rorty's ironists are people who
know that they exist in time because it is time and the changes it
brings that can make their former terminologies and their former
selves obsolete. Terms that serve your purposes one day will not
necessarily do so the next. The ironists' willingness to change
narratives, expand their circles of self, is something of a brave
act, in part because all awareness of existence in time is awareness of death. To follow the ironists' path is to admit to
mortality.

In trying to make contact with my students' Final Narratives, I
ask about more than religion. I ask about how they imagine the

good life. I ask, sometimes, how they picture their lives in ten years if all turns out for the best. I want to know what they hope to achieve in politics, in their professions, in family life, in love. Occasionally, I ask how they conceive of Utopia, the best of all possible worlds, or of Dystopia, the worst. But usually, for me, the matter of religion is present, a central part of the question.

There is nothing new about beginning a humanistic inquiry in this way. At the start of *The Republic*, Socrates asks his friends what they think justice is. And for Socrates, justice is the public and private state conducive to the good life. The just state and the just soul are mirror images of each other, comparably balanced. Socrates is quickly answered. Thrasymachus, aggressively, sometimes boorishly, insists that justice is the interest of the stronger. Socrates isn't put off by Thrasymachus, not at all. For Socrates recognizes that getting his students to reveal themselves as they are, or appear to themselves to be, is the first step in giving them the chance to change.

Posing the question of religion and the good life allows students to become articulate about who and what they are. They often react not with embarrassment or anxiety, but with surprise and pleasure, as if no one has ever thought to ask them such a question and they've never posed it to themselves.

But beginning here, with religion, also implies a value judgment on my part—the judgment that the most consequential questions for an individual life (even if one is, as I am, a longtime agnostic) are related to questions of faith. I also believe, for reasons I will get to later, that at this historical juncture, the matter of belief is crucial to our common future.

Most professors of the humanities have little interest in religion as a field of live options. Most of us have had our crises of faith early, if we've had them at all, and have adopted, almost as second nature, a secular vision of life. Others keep their religious commitments separate from their pedagogy, and have for so long that they're are hardly aware of it. But what is old to the teacher is new to the student. This question of belief matters greatly to the young, or at least it does in my experience. Asking it can break through the ideologies of training and entertaining. Beneath that veneer of cool, students are full of potent questions; they want to know how to navigate life, what to be, what to do. Matters of faith and worldliness are of great import to our students and by turning away from them, by continuing our treaty with the dispensers of faith where we tutor the mind and they take the heart and spirit, we do our students injustice.

We secular professors often forget that America is a religion-drenched nation. Ninety percent of us believe that God knows and loves us personally, as individuals. More than the citizens of any other postindustrial nation, we Americans attend church—and synagogue, and mosque. We affirm faith. We elect devout, or ostensibly devout, believers to the White House; recent presidents have been born-again Christians. Probably one cannot be elected president of the United States—cannot be our Representative Man—without professing strong religious faith. The struggle over whether America's future will be sacred or secular, or a mix of the two, is critical to our common future.

Some may well disagree with me about the centrality of religious matters, matters of ultimate belief, in shaping a true literary education. I teach in the South, one of the more religiously engaged parts of the nation, after all. Fine. But I think the point stands nonetheless. Get to your students' Final Narratives, and your own; seek out the defining beliefs. Uncover central convictions about politics, love, money, the good life. It's there that, as Socrates knew, real thinking starts.

Circles

RORTY IS A pragmatic philosopher, and like his pragmatic forebears Dewey and James, his preeminent task is to translate the work of Ralph Waldo Emerson into the present. Behind Rorty's reflections on Final Vocabularies, there lies one of the most profound passages that Emerson wrote. The passage is from the essay "Circles," and it stands at the core of the kind of literary education that I endorse.

In it Emerson brings forward a marvelous image for the way growth takes place in human beings, and perhaps, too, in society. The image he summons is that of the circle, the circle understood as an image of both expansion *and* confinement. "The life of man," he writes, "is a self-evolving circle, which, from a ring imperceptibly small, rushes on all sides outwards to new and larger circles, and that without end."

So far Emerson has made the process of human expansion seem almost automatic, as though it were a matter of natural evolutionary force. But, as is his habit, Emerson goes on to revise himself, expand himself through refinement. "The extent to which this generation of circles, wheel without wheel, will go, depends on the force or truth of the individual soul. For it is the inert effort of each thought, having formed itself into a circular wave of circumstance,—as, for instance, an empire, rules of an art, a local usage, a religious rite,—to heap itself on that ridge, and to solidify and hem in the life."

Emerson's insight is dialectical. Whatever gains we make in our knowledge of the self and the world, however liberating and energizing our advances may be, they will eventually become standardized and dull. What once was the key to life will become deadening ritual, common practice, a tired and tiresome Final Narrative. The critic Kenneth Burke is thinking of something similar when he talks about "the bureaucratizing of the imaginative"; Robert Frost touches on the point when he observes that a truth ceases to be entirely true when it's uttered even for the second time.

Emerson understands education as a process of enlargement, in which we move from the center of our being, off into progressively more expansive ways of life. We can see this sort of thing happening on the largest scale when the author of *Julius Caesar* becomes capable of creating the vast work that is *Hamlet*. Yet *Hamlet* is an outgrowth of *Caesar*; the character of Brutus expands—another circle on the great deep, if you like—into the revealing mystery that is Hamlet. But such rippling outward happens every day, too, as when a child leaves her family and goes out into the painful, promising world of school. Then the child's circle of knowing has to expand to meet the new circumstances, or she'll suffer for it.

The aim of a literary education is, in Emerson's terms, the expansion of circles. One's current circle will eventually "solidify and hem in the life." "But," Emerson immediately continues, "if the soul is quick and strong, it bursts over the boundary on all sides, and expands another orbit on the great deep, which also runs up into a high wave, with attempt again to stop and to bind. But the heart refuses to be imprisoned; in its first and narrowest pulses, it already tends outward with a vast force, and to intense and innumerable expansions."

This passage, eloquent as it is, breeds many questions. How shall we understand the substance of these expanding rings? What is their human content? How does one know that this or that new circle is conducive to better things than the old? Where does the impetus for enlargement come from? Is it always time to move outward, or is there a time in life when it makes sense to fall back, or to stand pat? What role do books have in this process? And what part does a teacher play? How does the student put herself in the way of the kind of expansion that Emerson describes? How does she know that it's coming to pass? Is it painful, pleasurable, both? Are such changes always for the better? Might they not also be changes for the worse?

For the purposes of literary education, I want to see these Emersonian circles as being composed of words. But the circles will also be alive with feeling. They will be rife with the emotions—the attractions and powers and taboos—that infuse the words that mean the most to us. Words like "mother" and "father" and "God" and "love" and "America" are not just blank counters in a game designed to fill up a stray hour. They are words with a history, personal and collective, words differently valued, differently felt, by each of us. We define them in ways partially our own, based on our experiences. And of course, the words also define us. So we might think of Emerson's circles as Rorty's Final Narratives. And we might think of the question about religion as a way to tap into one's ultimate terms, to make contact with one's outer-lying circles, and in so doing to initiate the process of growth.

It's time, no doubt, for a provisional thesis statement: the function of a liberal arts education is to use major works of art and intellect to influence one's Final Narrative, one's outermost circle of commitments. A liberal education uses books to rejuvenate, reaffirm, replenish, revise, overwhelm, replace, in some cases (alas) even help begin to generate the web of words that we're defined by. But this narrative isn't a thing of *mere* words. The narrative brings with it commitments and hopes. A language, Wittgenstein thought, is a way of life. A new language, whether we learn it from a historian, a poet, a painter, or a composer of music, is potentially a new way to live.

Grateful as I am for Rorty's translation and Emerson's luminous passage, there is one place where I must part company with them both (and with Allan Bloom as well). For my hopes, I think, are larger than theirs. I believe that almost anyone who has the opportunity to enjoy a liberal education—and such educations are not only to be had in schools; the world is full of farmers, tradesmen and tradeswomen, mechanics, lawyers, and, up to some crucial moment, layabouts, who've used books to turn their lives around—almost anyone is likely to be able to cultivate the power to look skeptically at his own life and values and consider adopting new ones. This ability—to expand one's orbits—is central to the health of democracy. The most inspired and inspiring Americans have always done so: others can and will join them. But the process is not an easy one. Allan Bloom is quite right: liberal education does put everything at risk and requires students who are willing to risk everything. Otherwise it can only touch what is uncommitted in the essentially committed student.

But Bloom, much, much more than Emerson and Rorty, believes that such risk and such change are only for the very few. Bloom sees Socrates' path as exclusively for an elite. It is not so.

For Ignorance

"WHAT THAT YOUNG man lacks is inexperience": so said the maestro of the young prodigy. Part of what I hope to do by asking students to brood publicly about God and ultimate commitments is to let them recapture their inexperience. They need a chance to own what may be the most precious knowledge one can have at the start of an education, knowledge of one's own ignorance.

Plato and Aristotle both say that philosophy begins in wonder. But Ludwig Wittgenstein, perhaps closer to the point, thought that people came to philosophy, to serious thinking about their lives, out of confusion. The prelude to philosophy was a simple admission: "I have lost my way." The same can be true for serious literary study. At its best, it often begins with a sense of dislocation; it begins with a sense that one has lost one's way.

The best beginning reader is often the one with the wherewithal to admit that, living in the midst of what appears to be a confident, energetic culture, he among all the rest is lost. This is a particularly difficult thing to do. For our culture at large prizes knowingness. On television, in movies, in politics, at school, in the press, the student encounters authoritative figures, speaking in self-assured, worldly tones. Their knowingness is intimidating. They seem to be in full command of themselves. They appear to have answered all the questions that matter in life and now to be left musing on the finer points. They demonstrate their preternatural poise by withholding their esteem. Not to admire anything, Horace said, is the only way to feel consistently good about yourself. Most of the cultural authorities now in place, in art, in the media, and in academia, are figures who programmatically hoard their esteem and apparently feel quite good about themselves in the process.

Should one believe in God? What is truth? How does one lead a good life? All these questions the cultural authorities appear to have resolved. Only the smaller matters remain.

But the true student has often not settled these matters at all.

Often she has not even come up with provisional answers that satisfy her. And finally, after years of observation and thought, she may be willing to wager that the so-called authorities probably haven't resolved them either. They're performing a charade, dispensing an unearned and ultimately feeble comfort. The true student demands more. And to find it, she is willing, against the backdrop of all this knowingness, to take a brave step. She is willing to affirm her own ignorance.

Beneath acculturation to cool, beneath the commitment to training and skills, there often exists this sense of confusion. And where it is, the student should be able to affirm it, and the teacher to endorse the affirmation.

"You must become an ignorant man again," says Wallace Stevens to his ephebe, or beginning poet. The same holds true for the beginning student of literature, and often for the teacher as well. The student must be willing to become as articulate as possible about what he has believed—or what he has been asked to believe—up until this point. He must be willing to tell himself who he is and has been, and, possibly, why that will no longer quite do. This exercise in self-reflection, deriving often from the sense of displacement, of having lost one's way, can start a literary education. And once a student has touched his ignorance, he has acquired a great resource, for in such ignorance there is the beginning of potential change—of new and confident, if provisional, commitment. As Thoreau puts it, "How can he remember well his ignorance—which his growth requires—who has so often to use his knowledge?"

Again and again, the true student of literature will return to this ignorance, for it's possible that no truth she learns in the humanities will be permanently true. At the very least, everything acquired by immersion in literature will have to be tested and retested along the way. It's for this reason that the teacher often enters a course with a sense of possibility akin to the students'.

One of the most important jobs a teacher has is to allow students to make contact with their ignorance. We need to provide a scene where not-knowing is, at least at the outset, valued more than full, worldly confidence. Thoreau heading to Walden Pond almost empty-handed, or Emily Dickinson going up to her room in Amherst to engage in a solitary dialogue with God, are grand versions of the kind of open and daring endeavor that we can all engage in for ourselves. Emerson says that power abides in transition, in "the shooting of the gulf, in the darting to an aim." We're most alive when we're moving from one set of engagements to the next. We're in motion then, but not fully sure where we're going, feeling both our present ignorance and the prospect of new, vitalizing knowledge.

Down the Hall

WHILE I'M ASKING my questions about God and what makes a good life, and affirming, when need be, a certain sort of ignorance, what's going on in the classrooms of my colleagues down the hall, and for that matter, in humanities classrooms across the country? A number of things, all well worth remarking upon. There is training, there is entertaining, no doubt. But many professors go at least some distance in resisting the ethos of the corporate university and of American culture overall. What they do can pass well beyond the university's ad brochures, where the students bask on the grass in all-approving sunlight, or hover around a piece of machinery that's high-tech, high-priced, and virtually unidentifiable.

Many professors of humanities—professors of literature and history and philosophy and religious studies—have something of consequence in common. Centrally, they attempt to teach one thing, and often do so with real success. That one thing is reading. They cultivate attentiveness to written words, careful consideration, thoughtful balancing, coaxing forth of disparate meanings, responsiveness to the complexities of sense. They try to help students become more like what Henry James said every writer ought to be, someone on whom nothing is lost. Attentiveness to words, to literary patterns and their meaning-making power: that remains a frequent objective of liberal arts education.

It was the New Critics who brought the phrase "close reading" to the fore in American education. Robert Penn Warren, Cleanth Brooks, William K. Wimsatt, and a number of other influential scholars pioneered an approach to reading that continues on, in various forms, into the present. The well-wrought students of Brooks and Warren were ever on the lookout for irony, tension, ambiguity, and paradox. To find these things, they had to scrutinize the page in front of them with exacting care. All to the good.

But what happens in most New Critical readings is that the master terms themselves—call them, if you like, elements in the New Critics' Final Narrative—take precedence over the actual poem. So rather than measuring the particular vision of John Donne, with all his manifold religious commitments and resistances, his sexual complexities, his personal kinks and quirks, the New Critic reworks Donne into a collection of anointed terms. Donne's "maturity"—to put matters in a compressed way—becomes a function of his capacity to cultivate paradox and irony.

Some writers are more responsive to New Critical values than others, and surely Donne is one of them. His work *is* replete with irony and ambiguity. Yet with the imposition of the rhetorical terms—terms that have no significant place in Donne's own Final Narrative—the poet becomes a function of New Critical values rather than a promulgator of his own.

The New Critical student, by encountering the right poems in the right way, undergoes a shaping, a form of what the Greeks called *paideia*. For the qualities that he learns to value in poems can also be cultivated in persons. So the ideal student (and the ideal professor) of New Criticism is drawn to the ability to maintain an ironic distance on life, the capacity to live with ambiguities, the power to achieve an inner tension than never breaks. The ideal New Critical student, like the ideal New Critical poem, is prone to be sophisticated, stoical, calm, intent, conventionally masculine, and rather worldly. What such a student is not likely to be is emotional, mercurial, rhapsodic, or inspired. The New Critical ethos—what we might call, after Keats, an ethos of negative capability, the capacity to be "in uncertainties, Mysteries, doubts, without any irritable reaching after fact & reason"—surely has its value. But it is one ethos among many. To reduce literature to that one ethos, when it contains a nearly infinite number, robs great writing of its diversity, and life of its richness.

The Harvard University scholar Walter Jackson Bate purportedly used a Marx Brothers style routine to capture what he thought of as New Critical close reading. "Close reading," he'd mutter, and push the book up near his nose. "Closer reading": with a laugh, digging his face down into the book. Then finally, "Very close reading," where nose and book kissed and not a word of print was legible. Bate's routine suggests that with a certain kind of exclusive attention to the page, life disappears. The connection between word and world goes dark (or becomes somewhat deviously implicit). The reader is left adrift, uncom-passed, in a sea of sentences.

Foucault, Industrial Strength

THERE WAS THIS much to be said for the New Critics: they were prone to specialize in reading and teaching works with which they were spiritually aligned. Donne and the New Critics genuinely do have something in common, though they also part company at important points. The violence of applying the anointed terms to Donne or Marvell or Keats's odes, or Shake-speare's sonnets is real, though hardly overwhelming. But down the hall in the humanities building now—and on the shelves of the library devoted to recent literary and cultural study—one finds work that is best described as out-and-out rewriting of the authors at hand. In fact, we might call these efforts not so much criticism as transformation.

Terry Eagleton, a Marxist critic drawing on the work of Pierre Macherey, describes a good deal of current criticism as quite simply an exercise in rewriting. One approaches the work at hand, and recasts it in the terms of Foucault, or Marx, or feminism, or Derrida, or Queer Theory, or what have you.

So a current reading of, say, Dickens's *Bleak House* is not so much an interpretation as it a reworking and a revision of the novel. Dickens is depicted as testifying, albeit unwittingly, to Foucault's major truths. In *Bleak House,* we are supposed to find social discipline rampant, constant surveillance, the hege-mony of the police, a carceral society. Whatever elements of the novel do not cohere with this vision are discredited, or pushed to the margin of the discussion. (In a Foucaultian reading of Shakespeare's *Henry IV,* Stephen Greenblatt, often a fine critic, manages to leave Falstaff virtually unmentioned.) Thus the critic rewrites Dickens in the terms of Foucault. One effectively reads not a text by Dickens, but one by another author. Dickens's truth is replaced by the truth according to Michel Foucault—or Fredric Jameson or Hélène Cixous—and there the process generally ends.

It may be that the truths unfolded by Foucault and the rest are of consummate value. It may be that those authors are indispensable guides to life, or at least to the lives of some. If so, all to the good.

If so, they, the critics, ought to be the objects of study in themselves. Let us look at Foucault, for instance, and see how one might lead a life under his guidance. What would you do? What would you do, in particular, as a denizen of an institution that produces precisely the kind of discipline that Foucault so detests? For a university, in Foucaultian thinking, is a production center, a knowledge-producing matrix which creates discourses that aid in normalizing people and thus in making them more susceptible to control. In fact, if you are a university citizen, you live in the belly of the beast. How, given what you've learned from Foucault, will you work your way out?

But these questions are virtually never asked. What usually happens is that professors apply the terminology to the work at hand, to Dickens or Emerson or Eliot, then leave it at that. The professor never measures the values and the shortcomings of the ruling critical idiom itself. For what authors who create comprehensive views of life offer is what Frost thought of as grand metaphors. "Great is he who imposes the metaphor," the poet said. But then it is the task of the reader, on encountering such metaphors, to see how far one can ride them out. At what point do they stop putting us in an illuminating relation to life? Where do they break down? Darwin's thinking about natural selection may help us to understand the animal kingdom. But should we use it to justify a society where all-out competition reigns? Perhaps this is a point where the grand Darwinian metaphor fractures.

Foucault would teach us that all disciplines discipline. That is, that every area of intellectual inquiry—psychology, sociology, history, literary criticism—tends toward providing reductive norms for human creations and for human behavior, thus delimiting possibility. Is this true? If so, what is there to do about it? What is there to do, in particular, if you are someone who, while using Foucault as the creator of your master narrative, at the same time is working in an institution, giving grades, collecting data, compiling reports, that effectively assault all that Foucault would seem to stand for?

This is not an unanswerable question. But surely it is the sort of question one must ask of one's own Final Narrative. In my experience, teachers of the humanities rarely do so. They rarely put the class's master terms on display, rarely make them the object of scrutiny and criticism.

If Foucault is your patron saint of wisdom (suggestive as I sometimes find him, he is not mine—to me he is a builder of dungeons in the air), then by all means bring him to the fore. Teach him directly. Let us see what language he has to unfold, what his Final Narrative entails. And if a language is also a way of life, we want to know what kind of life Foucault enjoins. A language, once taken on as an ultimate narrative, is not a set of markers, not merely a map, but a set of commitments, however contingent those commitments might be. It's necessary to test the author at hand, that is, as the source for a way of life.

When you apply Foucault to Dickens and don't turn in the direction of Foucault and interrogate his reach and value—his application to life—you lose what benefit Foucault may bring. When you translate Dickens into Foucault, you lose what benefit Dickens might have had to deliver. You leave with precious little, when there was so much that you might have had.

There is another disadvantage in applying theory to literature. To adapt a distinction made by Richard Poirier: literature tends to be dense; theory tends to be difficult. I can take my children, ages twelve and fourteen, to a production of *Hamlet*: no doubt they'll sleep through some of it, daydream through some more. But they'll also wake up at times—be shocked, puzzled, tickled, and occasionally illuminated. The best literature tends to be a layered experience. Even a beginning reader can get something from it. Then there's further to go, into legitimate complexity, true density and depth. Theory, on the other hand, tends to be an all-or-nothing affair. You get it or you don't. Face young people with a page of Derrida, whose reflections on the defining limits of Western thought are anything but valueless, and they're likely to depart with no benefit at all. Nothing is available for them. They don't get it, period. Then, once you've surmounted the difficulty, Derrida, like most theorists, tends to be a bit too available—theorists tend to have an astounding capacity to say the same thing over and over again.

If you set theory between readers and literature—if you make theory a prerequisite to discussing a piece of writing—you effectively deny the student a chance to encounter the first level of literary density, the level he's ready to negotiate. Theory is used, then, to banish aspiring readers from literary experience that by rights belongs to them.

The hasty reader might mistake my view for the "antitheory" position. For there are any number of professors of humanities who simply detest any and all far-reaching analytical work. I've written a book about contemporary theorists that's not at all unadmiring, and on occasion I teach their work. But experience has shown me that there are more viable and more varied options for students in literature itself, and that contemporary theory, though not without its appeals, tends to be implausibly extreme in its vision of experience and, accordingly, untenable as a guide to life. Can you live it? Alas, it's generally the case that no one can live out the latest version of theoretical apostasy and that, just as depressing, no one, even the theory's most devoted advocates, is even mildly inclined to try.

Interpretation

INTERPRETATION IS THE name of the game, says Stanley Fish, and all humanities professors must play. Fish is probably the best-known American literary critic at work today. His books on literary theory and on Milton are much consulted in the academy. To Fish, interpretation is a test of ingenuity. It's a way to demonstrate intellectual prowess. Often interpretation is a chance to push your reader's and student's credulity as far as possible, then a step further. Fish has observed that his aim as an interpreter is not to find truth but to be as interesting as he can be. Emphatically, the objective is not to make past wisdom available to the uses of the present, however badly such wisdom may be needed. For Fish, what literary critics do is inevitably without consequences: it changes nothing in academia or in the public world. Interpretation, for Fish, is a self-delighting and self-promoting game. He cites with full approval the view that "literary interpretation . . . has no purpose external to the arena of its practice; it is the 'constant unfolding' to ourselves 'of who we are' as practitioners; its audience is made up of those who already thrill to its challenges and resonate to its performances."

I suspect that Fish finds the seriousness with which he's regarded to be supremely amusing. I suspect that as a brilliant satirist unfolding one piece of performance art after another, he takes delight in pushing his academic readers as far into the ridiculous as possible. I've no doubt that Fish will be greatly relieved when people stop taking him literally, begin regarding him as the stern moralist that he actually is, and understand that he has always hoped we would do the opposite of what he recommended. In reading Fish on interpretation, one should become disturbed by one's own practice—by the practice of interpreting for the sake of interpreting, as something to do, because one is good at it, as a way to advance one's career—and try something better. By pretending to endorse things as they are, in their current near-absurdity, Fish is no doubt trying to stir professorial rebellion. But to Fish's probable surprise, professors have not seen that he is the closest thing the academy has to a Jonathan Swift.

But isn't it a good thing, this exercise of mind that students undergo when they interpret texts with ingenious rigor? Doesn't it strengthen the intellect, improve the powers of discernment, enhance capacities for what's called critical thinking?

Critical thinking is now much revered in humanities departments. We pride ourselves on dispensing it. But what exactly is critical thinking? Often it is no more than the power to debunk various human visions. It is, purportedly, the power to see their limits and faults. But what good is this power of critical thought if you do not yourself believe something and are not open to having these beliefs modified? What's called critical thought generally takes place from no set position at all. There is no committed vantage, however transient. Rather, one attacks from any spot that one likes, so everything is susceptible to denunciation. "One is clever and knows everything that has ever happened," as Nietzsche puts it in his passage on the Last Man, "so there is no end of derision." For the critical thinker there is no end of derision. When one thinks critically in behalf of creating a Final Narrative, that is something else again. Then you are sifting visions for their applications to life. A great deal is at stake. But most of what now passes as critical thinking takes place in a void.

In general, critical thinking is the art of using terms one does not believe in (Foucault's, Marx's) to debunk worldviews that one does not wish to be challenged by.

What happens when you teach critical thinking unattached to some form of ethics, or some process of character creation? What you help inculcate, I believe, is the capacity to use the intellect in ever more adroit ways. This kind of education does make the student smarter, in some abstract sense. It makes him more adept at the use of what the Frankfurt School thinkers liked to call instrumental reason. This sort of reason conceives the world in terms of problems and solutions. It is prone to abstraction, to the release of the intellect from the emotions, to extreme forms of detachment. The development of instrumental reason is good preparation for doing work in a corporation in which you look only at means and not at ends. You see processes, but not the ultimate performance. Then you go off, the better to enjoy Saturday night.

It may seem radical to be studying Foucault and Adorno. But students now do not study these figures, if by "study" we mean deciding after careful interpretation and long questioning whether the figures at hand have it right, whether the students ought to try to live with these writers as guides to life. On the contrary, students learn to apply the terms of analysis, like painters applying pigment to a house, or like systems analysts applying their standards to a particular disposition of persons and tasks. The values involved mean virtually nothing. You can be a close observer, you can write well, you can be brilliantly ingenious in making your terms appear to square with the poem at hand, you can even be someone on whom little or nothing is lost, and you can still be the sort of person who does what he is told without thinking much about it. You can still be someone who lives to follow orders.

What interpretation as currently taught encourages is a highly skilled, highly negotiable form of expertise that will often be prized by future employers in that it comes without inconvenient ethical baggage. Despite the rhetoric of subversion that surrounds it, current humanities education does not teach subversive skepticism (I wish that it did); rather, it teaches the dissociation of intellect from feeling—something that can be a prelude to personal and collective anomie. True education, as Friedrich Schiller rightly saw it, ought to fuse mind and heart. Current education in the liberal arts does precisely the opposite. At the end of this road lies a human type bitterly and memorably described in Weber: "Specialists without spirit, sensualists without heart; this nullity imagines that it has attained a level of civilization never before achieved."

"I'll die before I give you power over me," Narcissus liked to say to his many wooers, before he offended the goddess Hera and was forced to fall in love with his own image in a pool. The analysis of great works now often takes place beneath the auspices of Narcissus. The student is taught not to be open to the influence of great works, but rather to perform facile and empty acts of usurpation, in which he assumes unearned power over the text. Foucault applied at industrial strength is an automatic debunking agent. But the process leaves the student untouched, with no actual growth, just a reflexively skeptical stance that touches the borders of nihilism. Such activity, prolonged over the course of an education, is likely to contribute to the creation of what the philosopher James C. Edwards calls "normal nihilists." Normal nihilists are people who believe in nothing (except the achievement of their own advantage), and we may be creating them in significant numbers by not counting the ethical costs of our pedagogy. "It's easy to be brilliant," Goethe said, "when you do not believe in anything." And it's easy, too, to be brilliantly successful.

The sense of superiority that current liberal arts education often instills rhymes with some of the least creditable trends in our culture. It rhymes with a superior and exploitative relation to the natural world, with condescension to the poor, with a sense that nothing in the world matters unless it matters to Me. Analytic pedagogy, the pedagogy of instrumental reason, does not create these trends; far from it. But such pedagogy contributes to wrongs that it should be contending against.

What's missing from the current dispensation is a sense of hope when we confront major works, the hope that they will tell us something we do not know about the world or give us an entirely fresh way to apprehend experience. We need to learn not simply to read books, but to allow ourselves to be read by them.

And this process can take time. Describing his initiation into modern literature, into Kafka, Joyce, Proust, and their contemporaries, Lionel Trilling writes: "Some of these books at first rejected me; I bored them. But as I grew older and they knew me better, they came to have more sympathy with me and to understand my hidden meanings. Their nature is such that our relationship has been very intimate." "I bored them," says

Trilling. Given the form of literary education now broadly available, it is almost impossible that a student would say of a group of books, "I bored them." No, in the current consumer-driven academy another word, differently intoned, would be on the tip of the tongue: "Boooooooring." We professors have given our students the language of smug dismissal, and their profit of it is that they know how to curse with it and to curse those things that we ourselves have most loved and, somewhere in our hearts, probably love still.

Good at School

TRANSLATION HAS BEEN the order of the day for some time in the humanities, beginning with the relatively benign translations of the New Critics and moving on to the more and more strained recastings now current. The objective of humanistic study seems more and more to be the transformation of the best that has been known and thought into other, homogenizing languages, the languages of criticism, which we rarely take the time to interrogate or consider putting to use day to day.

When I entered graduate school in 1979 the reigning terms of translation were philosophical or, more accurately, antiphilosophical. These were the terms of deconstruction. When I was beginning at Yale, Paul de Man was working to propound a theory of antimeaning that he believed would have application to all of literature. From his point of view, writing that mattered culminated at points of undecidability. These are moments where two meanings come into play and it is impossible to make a determination as to which one supersedes the other. Undecidability is different from paradox, which is ultimately resolvable, and different too from oxymoron, in which the coupling of the terms reveals itself as an absurdity.

The end of Yeats's poem "Among School Children" asks us how we can know the dancer from the dance. The last four lines run this way:

> O chestnut-tree, great-rooted blossomer,
> Are you the leaf, the blossom or the bole?
> O body swayed to music, O brightening glance,
> How can we know the dancer from the dance?

To de Man, the final question is not resolvable. The poem at first seems to suggest that there is nothing so glorious as the moment when the dancer and the dance, form and experience, creator and creation merge. Thus the final line can be read as a celebration of full being outside of time. It's an affirmation of artistic transcendence. Yet, read somewhat differently, the poem also suggests that this moment may be illusory. Maybe we ought to take the last line literally rather than figuratively and try to figure out how we might actually achieve a skeptical detachment. Please instruct me: how *can* I separate the dancer from the dance? Perhaps the feeling of timelessness and interfusion is a delusory one that needs combating; perhaps it is conducive to feelings of omnipotence, to godlike illusions. It is desirable to know the dancer from the dance, for such knowledge might free us from mystification. Yet study the poem as one might, it does not affirm one reading at the expense of the other. So we are suspended between assurances, committed neither to one side nor the other.

De Man's larger argument is that literature perpetually yields these moments of unreadability. And herein lies the clinching point: this is what makes literature a particularly distinguished and enlightening form of discourse. Writes de Man, "A literary text simultaneously asserts and denies the authority of its own rhetorical mode." That capacity simultaneously to affirm and to deny is, according to de Man, really all that literature yields that is of consequence. People, human beings who in other regards were not noticeably brain befuddled, took this notion seriously.

It is reasonable to be attuned to such moments, to be sure (and I think Yeats does offer one here and that de Man explicates it shrewdly); and it can be illuminating to ponder them. This de Manian moment is not unrelated to Buddhist accounts of self-annulment, the achievement of egolessness through meditation. But Buddhists reflect constantly on the reasons for such a quest and on what might be achieved by a human being once the ego is annulled. In de Man, there is no such reflection on ends. His findings, such as they stand, are never put to existential work.

De Manian suspension between alternatives may be a good place to begin, or to rebegin, serious literary inquiry. But to imagine that such doubt is all that literature yields, or the best that literature yields, that all those marvelous books, marvelous vision, can be reduced to a moment that balances on the head of a pin, well, as Huck Finn put it, that's too many for me.

But de Man need not be singled out here. Rather, virtually every critic or school of criticism that matters has worked to reduce literary experience, vast and varied as it is, into a set of simple terms. They've turned contingent literature into delimiting philosophy (or, one might say, "metaphysics"), which says that there is one mode of happiness, one kind of good, one form of ideal life for everyone.

Salient in the process of transforming literary variety into philosophical uniformity has been psychoanalysis. For psychoanalysis lets the critic become a temporary therapist, diving into the inner life of the work, finding its hidden chambers, telling a story about the work and the author that the author could not herself tell. Now the power of the critic grows exponentially, as he configures himself as the wise analyst and the author as the patient, on the scene for needful therapy. Whatever the benefits of psychoanalysis to living patients who elect to become part of the process—and I think that they can be real—there is nevertheless little indication that psycho-literary analysis does anything for the patient. It does, however, enrich the analyst with no little power.

Why did these approaches, these forms of translation, catch on? For many reasons, not insignificant among them the teacher's will to power over the texts that she teaches. But these translating approaches work in part because they're good at school. They give the teacher something coherent to teach. They give the students a portable knowledge, something to take away from the scene. And they give them an illusion of potency over works far more potent than they. Current literary analysis allows students to take up the stance of cool complacency that they, and all of us, have become accustomed to from living in a spectatorial culture. The knowing literary-critical stance may be more difficult to achieve than the TV watcher's accustomed disdain, but the two positions are not unrelated. In both, one assumes an unearned and potentially debilitating superiority. We will not have real humanistic education in America until professors, and their students, can give up the narcissistic illusion that through something called theory, or criticism, they can stand above Milton, Shakespeare, and Dante.

If the latter-day Dionysus is the god of humanities entertainment, the new Apollo is the god of humanities analysis, the one who confers power and skills on his devotees. When you hear a literary critic repeating terms over and over, whether they be "ideology" and "class struggle," or "repression" and "neurosis," or "patriarchy" and "oppression," you know that you are in the hands of a writer who is devoted to the soft institutional usurpation of literary power, the better to create other, less varied kinds of writing—and fewer vital options.

Practitioners of all disciplines must promise something, implicitly or overtly. They tell their students that eventually they will possess a certain sort of knowledge. To thrive in a university, a department must promise some kind of desirable prowess, whether it be understanding of the physical world, knowledge of history's laws, or, in this case, a capacity to analyze and describe works of art as though they were species of fauna. We have made literary study fit in, be good at school. But true humanistic study is not geared to generalized, portable truths; it is geared to human transformation. And that is something that catalogues cannot describe and to which the writing of detached literary critical essays is more or less irrelevant.

Works that matter work differently. Such works, in history, philosophy, psychology, religious studies, and literature, can do many things, but preeminent among them is their capacity to offer truth. So far we've left the quest of truth to Falwell and to faith. We, the supposed heirs of Socrates, have fled from our authentic vocations. Perhaps it is time again to confront the Sphinx, who now, as always, poses the riddle of life: What use will you make of the world? (And what use might it make of you?) How do you intend to live? It is time, perhaps, to help our students look into the Sphinx's eye (and to look there ourselves); time to see what we see.

Truth

LITERATURE AND TRUTH? The humanities and truth?
Come now. What could be more ridiculous? What could be
more superannuated than that?
We read literature now for other reasons. We read to assert
ourselves, to sharpen our analytical faculties. We read to debunk
the myths. We read to know the other. We read, sometimes, for
diversion. But read for truth? Absurd. The whole notion of truth
was dispatched long ago, tossed on the junk heap of history
along with God and destiny and right and all the rest. Read for
truth? Why do that?

For the simple reason that for many people, the truth—the
circle, the vision of experience—that they've encountered
through socialization is inadequate. It doesn't put them into
a satisfying relation to experience. That truth does not give
them what they want. It does not help them make a contribution to their society. It does not, to advance another
step, even allow for a clear sense of the tensions between
themselves and the existing social norms, the prevailing doxa.
The gay boy can't accept the idea that his every third thought
is a sin. The visionary-in-the-making isn't at home with her
practical, earth-bound, and ambitious parents. Such people,
and I believe most people who go to literature and the liberal
arts out of more than mere curiosity are in this group,
demand other, better ways to apprehend the world—that
is, ways that are better *for them*. And the best repository
for those other ways are the works of the poets, as Williams
said, and of the painters and composers and novelists and
historians. Here one may hope for a second chance, a way to

begin the game again, getting it closer to right this time around.

But how do we find this truth? How do we begin to extract it from literature? Well, to begin with, we must read and interpret the work.

Here arises a problem. We all know that there is no such thing as a perfect interpretation. In fact, some of the more sophisticated among us have come to believe that interpretation is by necessity interminable. It's a mark of shallowness to believe that we can get to the core of the poem. Do I dare? Do I dare? So says the Prufrock of contemporary academia.

What I take to be worthwhile interpretation is centered on the author. I do not join my colleague E. D. Hirsch in affirming that the author's intention ought to be the measure of the reading at hand. We can never discover as much. There are simply too many levels of the mind that contribute to creation, not all of them responsive to analysis.

No, the art of interpretation is to me the art of arriving at a version of the work that the author—as we imagine him, as we imagine her—would approve and be gratified by. The idea is not perfectly to reproduce the intention; that can never be done. Rather, the objective is to bring the past into the present and to do so in a way that will make the writer's ghost nod in something like approval. That means operating with the author's terms, thinking, insofar as it is possible, the writer's thoughts, reclaiming his world through his language. In preparing to write *Fearful Symmetry*, Northrop Frye did all he could to merge with William Blake, to relive and in so doing to re-create his vision. And he did it with grand success.

The teacher's act of inspired ventriloquism need not be perfect. All that he needs to do is to supply a vision, based on the work at hand, that is as ramified as possible and that

offers a fertile alternative to what the students in class are likely
to believe, or are likely to believe that they believe.

But that's impossible, one might say. You can never satisfyingly reproduce an author's vision, or even come close. On the
contrary, we do this sort of thing all the time. We describe books
and films to each other. We use all the resources we can gather in
order to explain one friend to another. We recount situations of
almost unbearable complexity—the details of a long illness, the
dynamics of a divorce—in hopes of using our accounts to move
forward, to make the best of life, or what of life remains. Our
powers of description, which need not stop at paraphrase, are
often put to the test. They are among the most humanly
necessary powers we possess. Who should be in a better position
to deploy such powers than the professor who has been preparing for virtually all her life to do just that?

If this process of inspired re-rendering is impossible, why then
do we freely apply various theories to texts? Shouldn't the
impossibility of adequately apprehending *them* also offend
our sense of just complexity? If we can theorize about reading,
we can also evoke the experience of reading per se. All of the
punctilious rhetoric about the impossibility of rendering literature, of making contact with it and adding another voice to the
author's voice, illuminating what may be dark, making explicit
what is implicit, all of this resistance may be nothing more than
the timidity that stops us from turning a liberal arts education
from a field for mind-sharpening exercises, into what Keats
called a "vale of Soul-making."

The punctilious want perfect interpretation. They want to
score 100, as they have on all tests all of their lives. But what
presses us is too important to wait for perfection. What faces us
is the prospect of a world where religious meaning withdraws
and people are left in the midst of soul-destroying emptiness,

hopping and blinking and taking their little poison for the day and their little poison for the night.

A comparison with truth as it is apprehended in religion can be illuminating. As the scholar Karen Armstrong observes, "Modern New Testament scholarship has shown that we know far less about the historical Jesus than we thought we did. 'Gospel truth' is not as watertight as we assumed. But this has not prevented millions of people from modeling their lives on Jesus and seeing his path of compassion and suffering as leading to a new kind of life. Jesus certainly existed, but his story has been presented in the Gospels as a paradigm."

The Gospels do not capture Jesus perfectly; the readers of the Gospels presumably do not capture their essence to perfection, should such perfection exist. But that has not stopped many people from having their lives changed—and to their perception, changed for the better—through encounter with Jesus and his much-mediated word.

The test of an interpretation is not whether it is right or perfect, but whether it leads us to a worldview that is potentially better than what we currently hold. The gold standard is not epistemological perfection. The gold standard is the standard of use.

Wordsworth's Truth

WHAT DOES IT mean to ask of a poem if it is true? What are we taking a poem—or any work of human intellect and imagination—to be, if it is potentially a source of truth? Why don't we follow Kant, and all the idealists before and after him, in seeing art as purely disinterested? Why are we unable to concur with Sir Philip Sidney in his oft-cited view that

the poet "nothing affirms and therefore never lieth"? Why not
artistic purity? Why not art as purposiveness without any
specific purpose?

What I am asking when I ask of a major work (for only major
works will sustain this question) whether it is true is quite simply
this: Can you live it? Can you put it into action? Can you
speak—or adapt—the language of this work, use it to talk to
both yourself and others so as to live better? Is this work
desirable as a source of belief? Or at the very least, can it
influence your existing beliefs in consequential ways? Can it
make a difference?

Let us say that the work at hand is Wordsworth's "Lines
Composed a Few Miles Above Tintern Abbey On Revisiting the
Banks of the Wye During a Tour. July 13, 1798." The poem—it
is anything but accidental—takes place not far away from a
ruined abbey. In the midst of the ruins of religion—or the ruins
of *conventional* religious prospects for him—Wordsworth finds
himself forced to compound a new faith. This faith will not be
based on preexisting scripture; it will not be a faith received from
others. Wordsworth, spurred on by his return to a scene that was
at the center of his childhood, will gather to himself those
memories that give him the power to go on living and go on
writing.

The world as Wordsworth has lately experienced it is stale,
flat, and profitless. He lives in a din-filled city, among unfeeling
people—and, worse yet, he senses that he is becoming one of
them. He thinks of himself as abiding "In darkness and amid the
many shapes / Of joyless daylight." Time upon time, he says,
"the fretful stir / Unprofitable, and the fever of the world, / Have
hung upon the beatings of my heart." There is a dull ache settling
into his spirit, one that the eighteenth century would have called
melancholy and we would now call depression. But rather than

relying on religious consolation, as Dr. Johnson tried to do when he battled his own terrible despondency, or on drugs, as Wordsworth's dear friend Samuel Taylor Coleridge did, Wordsworth relies on himself. Laudanum, predecessor of today's antidepressant drugs, the serotonin reuptake inhibitors, and Coleridge's preferred source of solace, is not what's wanted. The poet will find consolation in himself or not at all.

And why should he not be disconsolate? For how can one bear life in its manifold sorrows, with all of its horrible sufferings, the sufferings of children and the innocent preeminent among them (think of the horrors unfolding in the world as you read this page, as I write it) and not go mad? Virtually all of us are bound to suffer as well—"pain of heart, distress, and poverty," if not of one sort then of another, to use Wordsworth's phrasing from "Resolution and Independence." But what seems to trouble Wordsworth most is that amidst this commonality of suffering, we still treat one another with rank callousness, with "greetings where no kindness is," "rash judgments," "sneers." Without the figure of a loving (or at least a just) God presiding over the world, ready at some point to dispense rewards to the worthy, and punishment or correction to the erring, it is no easy matter to find a reason not to despair. Where is Wordsworth, who seems devoid of religious faith (pious Coleridge always feared for Wordsworth's soul) to find any reason to continue on?

Wordsworth's answer is that there is a part of himself that is free from the fallen society in which he's immersed. It is a part that lives on deep in him, although covered over by custom, convention and fear. And in this region of half-remembered being he finds hope, or, as he puts it, "life and food / for future years."

He remembers himself as a child free in nature, with a spirit that belongs to nothing but the gorgeous, frightening natural world and has not been colonized by the city and its dispiriting ways. He thinks of the time "when first / I came among these hills; when like a roe / I bounded o'er the mountains, by the sides / Of the deep rivers, and the lonely streams, / Wherever nature led." In memories of that free self, Wordsworth finds an authentic pleasure, a vision of life lived without the anxieties that attend on awareness of death. The child in Wordsworth is free of that mortal fear; he senses that he will return painlessly to the natural world that brought him forth and gave him his vital, unambiguous force.

There is something in the poet that was there before civilization left its imprint. That something is free and it makes Wordsworth freer, however temporarily. In the last phase of the poem, he worries, edging again toward gloom, about whether in time the freedom will be foreclosed. He is becoming aware, in other words, of the merely transitory power that Emerson associated with even the most impressive human expansions. In time, they can "solidify and hem in the life." Maybe this contact with nature existing inside of him won't serve Wordsworth as an antidote all his life through.

Some critics like to look at this poem as a major moment in "the Romantic invention of childhood." But that is too ironic and distancing a notion. For the poem asks us to look into our own childhoods and into the lives of the children around us, and to see if they might not have something to teach us. May they show us how to live in a less guarded, more joyous and exuberant way? Could they teach us how, for a while, to stanch our fears of the future, and live in the present moment in nature? ("We are blessed always if we live in the present," says the American Wordsworthian, Thoreau.)

And what about this nature? The poem asks us to look around

at nature as it exists in our moment, and to consider what sort of restoration is to be found there. It suggests that in nature is the perpetuation of human vitality, that between civilization and nature there is a dialectic, and that letting one element in the tension grow too mighty, as Wordsworth's eighteenth-century forebears seem to the poet to have done, can be killing. This poem has legitimate connections to the best current ecology movements. The work can add to—or create—the conviction that in the love of wilderness and its preservation, there lies hope for humanity.

In "Tintern Abbey," one also encounters the bracing hypothesis that depression or melancholia or what-have-you is a great force, to be sure, but that it is a force we may combat through individual resourcefulness and faith. Maybe the answer to one's despondency does not lie in nature or memory or childhood per se, but Wordsworth's poem enjoins us to feel that it lies somewhere within our own reach. The site of our sufferings, what J. H. Van den Berg called the overfilled inner self, may also be the source of our cure. We are creatures who have the capacity to make ourselves sick, collectively and individually, but we often have the power to heal ourselves as well.

All these things, and many more besides, readers may draw from "Tintern Abbey." They may say, "Yes, of course, I've always thought so, but never quite had the words to say as much." Or "All right, I'll try Wordsworth's cure, or something like it. It could very well work." Others will be put off by this particular vision. Perhaps they'll find it too self-absorbed. Where are the others? What is Wordsworth to give to the poor? What is Wordsworth's role in the larger human hope for liberation or freedom from want? These are valuable questions. And if the answers—and there are answers—do not satisfy the individual reader, then he will legitimately look for another place to put his allegiances, another circle to expand into. Or perhaps he will stay with some enhanced confidence in his own.

But asking critical questions should not devolve into a mere parlor game. That is, we should not teach our students that the aim of every reading is to bring up the questions that might debunk the wisdom at hand, then leave it at that. We must ask the question of belief. Is this poem true? Can *you* use this poem? Or are you living in a way that's better than the poem suggests you might live? To these queries, we should expect only heartfelt answers.

By refusing to ask such questions once we have coaxed the work's vision forward, we are leaving our students where we found them. And if we leave them in the grasp of current social dogma, we are probably leaving them in the world of the normal nihilist; we are leaving them to the ideology of the consumer university, center of training and entertaining, in its worst manifestations. We may turn "Tintern Abbey" into a species of diversion, or we may turn it into an occasion for acquiring analytical techniques, but in doing so we are mistaken. For there is a deep force in the poem that we can put to saving uses in the present.

We ask often what we think of great works. What, we might also ask, would the creators of those works think of us? What would the Wordsworth of "Tintern Abbey," replete with drawbacks though that poem may seem to some, think of our posturing analytics?

But, one might say, all I have produced here is a reading, itself a translation of Wordsworth, no different from the application of, say, Foucault's terms to Wordsworth's poem. Isn't that right?

I don't think so.

Granted, my account of Wordsworth would not match the

poet's own, word for word. Granted, there are points at which, brought to life to listen, the poet might part company with the description at hand (or with the more expansive account of the work that I would offer in a classroom). But I have tried to be true to the poem. I have attempted, acting something like its advocate before the court of readers' opinion, to make the best possible case for its application to life. And as a teacher I have done so, in fact I must do so, as though I believed in the poet's every word.

The fact is that I do not. I may want, in time, to register my quarrels with this vision of experience, and I may want to offer the criticisms of others. But before those criticisms arrive, the poem needs to have its moment of maximum advocacy; it requires, and by its power it has earned, a display of full faith. And the testament to that faith takes place in a language integrally related to the language of Wordsworth. The teacher speaks of nature and childhood and memory. And that is a much different thing from speaking of discipline and norms and discourses, as Foucault might do in the face of this work. There is a difference between evocative description and what Eagleton and Macherey call rewriting. Both reimagine the work. Both bring the past into the present. But the difference in approach is so great as to constitute not a difference in degree, but a difference in kind. One is re-presentation, one translation.

The activity I have in mind is in some regards anticipated by Nietzsche's precursor in philosophy, Arthur Schopenhauer. "What is life?" That, to Schopenhauer, is the question at the core of all consequential art works. Schopenhauer believes that "every genuine and successful work of art answers this question in its own way with perfect correctness." The reader's task is to bring the works' wisdom to the fore: "The works of the poets,

sculptors, and representative artists in general contain an unacknowledged treasure of profound wisdom. . . . Everyone who
reads the poem or looks at the picture must certainly contribute
out of his own means to bring that wisdom to light; accordingly
he comprehends only so much of it as his capacity and culture
admit of; as in the deep sea each sailor only lets down the lead as
far as the length of the line will allow." For Schopenhauer,
however, the artists reveal one major truth and one only, that of
the Life Will in its sublime potency. To us now, literature, and
the arts in general, reveal truths that are multiple. Every artist
that matters gives us a world of words that we may translate into
a world of acts. Poets, to modify Shelley a little, are the too often
unacknowledged legislators of the word.

Professional literary critics shy away from the process I have
been describing, in part because they fear they can never get
the poem exactly right, never render it into the present in a
way that would satisfy some abstract standard of perfection.
But perfection is not at issue here. What we really need to do is
to use Wordsworth as the basis for constructing and conveying
a Final Narrative, a way of seeing and saying things, which is
potentially better than what our students or readers possess.
Your visions being true to every moment in the poem is less
important than that you offer live options to those around you.
The chances are that as a teacher, you will need a Wordsworth
to offer such vital options—you will need a visionary's help.
You and I will not be able to do so on our own. And so the
vision will be much more Wordsworth's than ours. But the key
is to offer our students something potentially better than what
they have, and to see if it resonates with their own best
aspirations.

Identification

THE QUESTIONS I pose about "Tintern Abbey" and about virtually every other work of art are inseparable from the matter of identification. That is, I ask students to perform a thought experiment. I ask them to use their powers of empathy and imagination to unite with another being. In the case of "Tintern Abbey," the being is the poet, but I have no qualms about asking readers to identify themselves with characters in novels, with Pip in *Great Expectations*, with Isabel Archer in *The Portrait of a Lady*, with Rastignac in *Old Goriot*, with Emma in Jane Austen's novel. I often ask them to find themselves, or to discover what is unknown in themselves, among the great characters in literature as well as within the imaginations that bring those characters to life.

Discussing James's *Portrait of a Lady*, I begin with a simple question. Does James love Isabel Archer?

Almost all of my students do. They find her vital, benevolent, charming, a full embodiment of what is best about America. They're drawn to her verve and her courage, particularly at the start of the book when she is young and on her own and, with an American insouciance, refusing offers of marriage from one Old World potentate after the next. They love Isabel, often, because in her they see their own best selves. They identify with all that is freshest and most promising in her.

Almost as a reflex my students tend to take the next step: James must love his heroine, too. They all love Isabel, after all, and in loving Isabel love some part of themselves. Surely James concurs.

But then we begin to read the novel—that is, to interpret it—

and some surprising things happen. James's disdain for his heroine, which is not unalloyed with considerable affection, is there on the page nearly from the start. In lengthy, authoritative, and summary accounts he attacks her with the greatest force. It's clear that he detests what he takes to be her shallowness, her glib self-confidence, her habit of thinking far too highly of herself. James writes that Isabel "had no talent for expression and too little of the consciousness of genius; she only had a general idea that people were right when they treated her as if she were rather superior." And later in the same passage: "Her thoughts were a tangle of vague outlines . . . In matters of opinion she had had her own way, and it had led her into a thousand ridiculous zigzags. At moments she discovered she was grotesquely wrong, and then she treated herself to a week of passionate humility. After this she held her head higher than ever again; for it was of no use, she had an unquenchable desire to think well of herself." James can admire Isabel, too; he is far too fine a novelist to give us a simple portrait. But his dislike for her American egotism at many points reaches contempt.

In a sense, Isabel's horrid fate, marriage to the disgusting, fortune-seeking Gilbert Osmond, is James's punishment for her. In terms of novelistic probability, the marriage seems rather forced. What we see of the courtship falls far short of persuading us that Isabel would actually give in and marry Osmond. But a purgative marriage—a punishment—is what Isabel needs, so the master of realistic fiction bends plausibility and brings it to pass. Isabel's small-time hubris, the vanity of provincial America, summons Gilbert Osmond and the almost equally appalling Madame Merle to deliver to Isabel the chastening that, as I believe James sees it, she so deserves. Brash Isabel early in the book announces that she might rather go without clothes than be defined by them. By the end, James has her dressed in so many layers of drapery that the four-piece suit Woolf said T. S. Eliot favored looks liberating by contrast. And then James is content, for Isabel has been chastened. She has learned to submit. She has learned to surrender her American wildness in the interest of something else, something more European and refined and more modestly fitted to an awareness of human limits. Then James does admire her—her submission to fate is rather awful and rather touching. One recalls the sufferings that the Marquis de Sade visits on the unworldly, Rousseauian Justine, whose naive sense of human nature the Divine Marquis despises. It may not be going too far to say that in *Portrait* James is our Marquis, and Isabel is the one whose virtue finds its reward. What James detests in this novel and chastens with purgatorial zeal is the American wildness to be found in Emerson, in Whitman (whom James notoriously poked fun at), and in Emily Dickinson. That the spark should be alive in a woman is probably all the more frightening to James.

The first time I discussed this book in class I was surprised by the result. Most of the students were outraged that, on reasonably close examination, it was clear that James's sentiments about the young Isabel were, to put it kindly, critical. What made this perception particularly difficult is that those harsh Jamesian sentiments had now to be seen as in some measure about them, about their own possible naïveté, about their own unthinking self-love—that is, about the aspect of themselves that they had discovered in Isabel. Many declared themselves anti-Jamesian. "Henry James must be one of the cruelest authors ever to write," one essay began. They saw James, I believe accurately, as the enemy of a certain kind of American spirit—though by no means an unambivalent enemy.

But a few of the students felt differently. What they came to believe was that Isabel needed to be chastened. She deserved it.

She had found her apt fate as surely as a protagonist in a Greek tragedy finds his. Osmond was exactly what she needed and exactly what she deserved so as to "suffer into truth," to use a Sophoclean formulation. Two of the students were candid enough, and brave enough, to say that, in fact, they felt that the harsh discipline that James was applying to Isabel ought well to be applied to them. They were like Isabel Archer in her earliest manifestation, and like her needed submission to purgatorial cleansing. As the book burned away what was most noxiously self-assertive in Isabel, so they hoped that it might do the same for them. Or at least it might begin the process. Such puritanical resolve on the part of early twenty-first-century American students struck me as both a little frightening and quite moving.

As someone who far prefers Emerson to James, indeed who prefers the young Isabel to James, as a temperament, I was temporarily saddened that people so young could be drawn to puritanical self-dislike. But I soon saw that my response was neither here nor there. It didn't much matter. I had done my job, which was to put students in a position to read and then to be read by the work at hand. Everyone who sat through that class was in a position to know himself better by virtue of the exchange. In this discussion, the process of "identification," of seeing oneself in a literary character, was essential.

Few activities associated with literary study are in worse repute than identification. Teachers in middle school—grades six to eight—by now caution against it, seeing it as a block to serious study. Surely it has no place in a college classroom. Surely no professor should endorse it publicly.

Sometimes what worries teachers about identification is the belief that it's inseparable from wish-fulfillment. You become one with a heroic figure and leave your small, timid self behind.

What you have then is a mere daydream. I find both wish-fulfilling fantasies, as literature provides them, and daydreaming to be precious human activities, for reasons that I'll later explain. But the process of identification that went on with Isabel—by young men and by women both—was not a matter of wish-fulfillment. On the contrary, in the identification process any simple narcissism underwent serious challenge by James. This is so because in studying James, as in studying any consequential writer, the step that follows identification is analysis of a firm but generous sort.

Still there's something about the process that can make the professional critic squirm. Perhaps it's the release of emotion that's involved, the fact that when we work with identification we don't sound like scientists who command a rigorous disci-pline. Perhaps we don't sound official or academic enough. Maybe we're worried about our authority. But as inspired religious teachers and artists of every stripe demonstrate all the time, the process of human growth—when it entails growth of the heart as well as of the mind—is never particularly clean or abstract. To grow it is necessary that all of our human qualities come into play, and if some of those qualities are not pretty, then so be it. But to keep them to the side so as to preserve our professional dignity—that is too much of a sacrifice. (Men and women die every day, perish in the inner life . . . for lack of what we have to offer.)

In general, academic literary study over the past two decades has become ever colder and more abstract. But there is one area of exception. Many feminist teachers have been willing to deal with emotion and the facts of daily life in their classrooms. Against prevailing orthodoxies, these professors have insisted on speaking personally, and have made sure that their students have had a chance to do so. Some feminists, it's true, have surrendered to pressure for high-toned theoretical respectability, but many have stuck to their guns and talked intimately and immediately about experience. It's in classrooms of this sort that students can at times connect the books they read to their own lives. Something similar can be true in classes on race, at least when students can talk candidly. (For a variety of complex reasons, though, they almost never can be direct and honest on this subject, even with the best-intentioned professors presiding.) But such classrooms are, alas, just about the only places where bringing together word and world is still the objective.

Milan Kundera speaks about novels as being populated by "experimental selves." These selves are persons whom we might be or become, or who signify aspects of the self. The novelist— with our assistance—sends them forth into the world, to see what the world will make of them, and they of it. They are the fictive human embodiments of what Nietzsche would call thought experiments. These selves are not after a long-lasting truth. Rather, they engage in an inquiry; they try, in good Emersonian fashion, to expand their particular orbits on the deep, sometimes successfully, sometimes not. Dickens's Pip needs to surrender his great expectations and expand into a life of humane, well-measured decency; Austen's Emma needs to see that the world has more living and feeling beings in it than herself and those few she holds in high regard. But part of what those characters learn is that no way of seeing things is final. They don't look, and cannot look, for a final resting place sanctioned by a larger authority than themselves. As Kundera puts it, "The world of one single Truth and the relative, ambiguous world of the novel are molded of entirely different substances. Totalitarian Truth excludes relativity, doubt, questioning; it can never accommodate what I would call the *spirit of the novel.*"

The rise of the novel coincides with a realization expressed, or perhaps created, by the development of democracy. That realization is of the great span of individuals to be found in the world, of the sheer proliferation of divergent beings. The commonplace that we each have a novel within us actually touches a consequential truth. It suggests that there are as many mysteries, as many ways of being, as there are lives. Whitman asserts this idea by being a deeply inward lyric poet who also recognizes the divergence of human lives around him—the balance he strikes between the intensity of the personal lyric and the breadth of the novel is part of what makes him a major figure, and one who speaks to the movement of his times. I think that a humanistic education begins in literature because, unlike philosophy, literature does not assume that one or two or five paths are enough to offer human beings. There are too many of us, and we are all too different; we all have our open-ended truths to pursue.

Gender and Identification

As I mentioned, some of the students who identified themselves with Isabel Archer were male. They did not read as men. Rather they read as human beings, finding in Isabel some of their own griefs and hopes. More and more I see this happening.

I frequently teach the *Iliad*, generally derided as the most outmoded of books, something to be tossed onto the junk heap of history. When I was teaching as a graduate student at Yale, the book was chiefly considered as an opportunity to reflect on the way that women were regarded in the Homeric period, and then to reflect on how much had changed or was changing.

Is the *Iliad* a book replete with vital possibilities, or is it a mere historical curiosity? Is it locked in the past, or a potent guide to the present and the future? A number of my students—men and women both—initially thought that it was a period piece and nothing more. The way the poem treated women disgusted them. In the *Iliad*, they said, a woman has the status of a few bullocks or a bronze tripod or two. True. Some, like Helen, are beautiful, and that beauty is a sort of power, but it is a limited, debased power compared to what the men wield. This is all well worth saying, well worth pointing out.

What the men have is the heroic life, with all its possibilities for glory. As C. M. Bowra describes it: "The essence of the heroic outlook is the pursuit of honour through action. The great man is he who, being endowed with superior qualities of body and mind, uses them to the utmost and wins the applause of his fellows because he spares no effort and shirks no risk in his desire to make the most of his gifts and to surpass other men in his exercise of them. His honour is the centre of his being, and any affront to it calls for immediate amends. He courts danger gladly because it gives him the best opportunity of showing of what stuff he is made. Such a conviction and its system of behaviour are built on a man's conception of himself and of what he owes to it, and if it has any further sanctions, they are to be found in what other men like himself think of him. By prowess and renown he gains an enlarged sense of personality and well-being; through them he has a second existence on the lips of men, which assures him that he has not failed in what matters most. Fame is the reward of honour, and the hero seeks it before everything else."

The class was about ready to concur that such a worldview was a thing of the past, or should best be, when one of the women students, usually quiet, spoke up. She said that the poem mattered to her because she could see things from Achilles' point of view. The moment that caught her attention first was the one in which Achilles' father tells him that he must be the best in every undertaking. He can simply never accept the second place. "I'm an athlete," she said, "and that's how I was raised by my parents and my coaches. I was told that I had to win at everything. I had to come in first all the time. After a while, though, I had to stop living like that. It's too much."

"Have you ever wanted to go back to it?" someone asked.

"Yes," she said, "all the time. It makes life incredibly intense." By which she meant, I suppose, that such a life provides ongoing energy; it allows for full, unambivalent human exertion, in the midst of a culture that often encourages self-dividing responses. If Wordsworth's meditative return to childhood is one viable answer to melancholia, then surely unbridled competitiveness is another. Competition can be a way to give what's vital in you more life. You could see that what had once been closed off and left behind for this student began to open again. The life of competition, the *agon*, is not for everyone, and it will not be approved by all. But if it is your highest aspiration, the thing you most want, then, whether you take the path or not, it is worth knowing about your attraction to it. Homer's heroic life is the life of *thymos*, the thirst for glory, and if you are, at whatever depths, an individual driven by *thymos*, by the desire for glory and praise, despite the moral censors you've thrown up against that drive, you need to deal with the fact in one way or another. I know no better way to begin doing so than through Homer.

Another classroom scene can help to illustrate the kind of teaching I want to endorse. A student in the same class, a young African-American woman, professes in her opening essay on the good life to be an ardent Christian. She believes in doing unto others as you would have them do unto you, in turning the other cheek. She believes Jesus to be the most perfect of mortals. But she reads the *Iliad* and, after a period of indifference, she's galvanized by it. What sweeps her in is a life where triumph matters above all else. She is fascinated by the fact that the warriors in the poem always seek victory. Envy is not a vice to them; it goads them to glories. The young woman, who, it comes out, wants to be a well-to-do corporate lawyer, has no trouble seeing some of herself in the unapologetic ambitions of Homer's heroes.

But then, too, she wants to be a Christian? Jesus' originality lies partly in his attempt to supersede admiration for the ambition and self-vaunting of Homer's heroes—an admiration very much alive in the Roman empire Jesus is born into. Which will it be, my student needs to ask herself, Jesus or Achilles?

Of course, what she really needs is a live synthesis of the two. And it is her task to arrive at it. But without the encounter with Homer, and without our raising the simple and supposedly elementary question of identification—Is there anything in you that is Achillean?—she might not have had access to her own divided state. With such self-knowledge achieved, she is in a position for productive change. This was an instance not only of reading and interpreting a book—we spent a long time coming to understand the heroic code and considering Homer's highly equivocal attitude toward it—but of allowing the book to interpret and read the reader.

Some teachers say that we must teach books like the *Iliad* because they show us a world so different from our own that it presses the values of this, our world, into sharp contrast. On the contrary, I teach the *Iliad* because in many significant ways, Homer's world is ours, though we are not always able to see as much immediately. In a passing remark about Homer, Nietzsche observes that part of what makes his world hard to assimilate for moderns is that to Homer's heroes, jealousy is not a negative emotion, not a feeling to be suppressed. Rather, one's desire for the first place is proudly announced. One revels in the hunger for dominance. In a culture where pagan values contend with Christian values—that is to say, in our culture—often the Christian aspirations to modesty and grace serve to cover over lust for glory and other kindred drives. Reading Homer can peel the cover back and allow us to see ourselves as we are. This great book—among the greatest and the most disturbing in the Western tradition—is anything but a period piece. Rather, it is a book that lives very much in the present. It is news that stays news, to cite Ezra Pound's still valuable, still newsworthy description of what makes literature literature.

Yet exactly how far is one to go in expanding literary meanings to make them apt for the present and future? It's unlikely that Homer ever imagined a pervasive cult of the warrior, however sublimated, that would be comprehensively open to women. By what right do I, or my students, enlarge his sense to fit our needs? I think that, having established the author's vision, insofar as it's possible, and having been as true to him as, say, Bowra seems to me to be true to an aspect of Homer, we are free to enlarge the work, always being aware of what it is we do. The test of the reading that leaves the provinces of the author's vision is use. What can we do with this work? What aspects of our lives does it illuminate? What action does it enjoin? We test the work, then, against the template of experience, as my students did. They wondered what would happen to them if they brought Homer's vision to life here and now. The ultimate test of a book, or of an interpretation, is the difference it would make in the conduct of life.

But Shakespeare?

DOES THE WORK contain live options? Does it offer paths one might take, modes of seeing and saying and doing that we can put into action in the world? How, in other words, does the vision at hand, the author's vision, intersect with—or combat—your own vision of experience, your own Final Narrative?

Do you want to second Wordsworth's natural religion? It's not a far-fetched question at a moment when many consider ecological issues to be the ultimate issues on the world's horizon. Is it true, what Wordsworth suggests in "Tintern Abbey" about the healing powers of Nature and memory? Can they fight off depression? Not an empty question in an age when antidepressant drugs have become unbearably common. Is Milton's Satan the shape that evil now most often takes—flamboyant, grand, and self-regarding? Or is Blake's Satan—a supreme administrator, mild, bureaucratic, efficient, and congenial, an early exemplar of Hannah Arendt's "banality of evil"—a better emblem? Or, to strike to the center of the tensions that often exist between secular and religious writing, who is the better guide to life: the Jesus of the Gospels, or the Prometheus of Percy Bysshe Shelley, who learned so much from Christ, but rejected so much as well—in particular Jesus' life of celibacy?

All right, one might say, but those are Romantic writers, polemicists, authors with a program. Even Henry James might be considered part of this tradition, albeit as an ambivalent anti-Romantic. What about other writers? What about, for instance, the famous poet of negative capability, who seems to affirm nothing, William Shakespeare? The most accomplished academic scholars of Shakespeare generally concur: they cannot tell what Shakespeare believed about *any* consequential issue. How can you employ Shakespeare in a way of teaching that seeks to answer Schopenhauer's question "What is life?" And if you can make nothing of Shakespeare, greatest of writers, then what value could this approach to literature, this democratic humanism as we might call it, possibly have?

If Sigmund Freud drew on any author for his vision of human nature—right or wrong as that vision may be—it was Shakespeare. The Oedipus complex, to cite just one instance of Freud's Shakespearean extractions, might just as well be called the Hamlet complex, as Harold Bloom has remarked. From Shakespeare, Freud might also have gathered or confirmed his theories of sibling rivalry; of the tragic antipathy between civilization and the drives; of bisexuality; of patriarchal presumption; of male jealousy; of all love as inevitably being the love of authority; of humor as an assault on the superego; and a dozen more psychoanalytical hypotheses. Shakespeare may not have affirmed these ideas out and out—he is not, it's true, a polemicist in the way that Blake is. But the question remains: Does Shakespeare/Freud work? Does their collaboration, if it is fair to call it that, illuminate experience, put one in a profitable relation to life, help you live rightly and enjoy your being in the world?

Readers of Freud's *Group Psychology and the Analysis of the Ego* will recall the daunting image of the leader Freud develops there. The leader, from Freud's point of view, is a primal father. In him the crowd places absolute trust, the trust of the child as it was aimed at his own father early on in life. Here is how Freud describes the primal and primary figure: "The members of the group were subject to ties just as we see them today, but the father of the primal horde was free. His intellectual acts were strong and independent even in isolation,

and his will needed no reinforcement from others . . . He loved
no one but himself, or other people only in so far as they
served his needs. To objects his ego gave away no more than
was barely necessary . . . Even to-day the members of a group
stand in need of the illusion that they are equally and justly
loved by their leader; but the leader himself need love no one
else, he may be of a masterful nature, absolutely narcissistic,
self-confident and independent."

In Shakespeare, whose work he read intensely from early on
in life to the end, Freud could have seen precisely such a
dynamic of leadership unfold. When we first encounter Prince
Hal, later to become the mighty Henry V, he seems to be
something rather different from the leader that Freud describes. He is mischievous, witty, and dissolute, and bosom
friends with the prince of dissipation, Sir John Falstaff. In the
three plays in which Hal appears, developing into King Henry
V, we see a metamorphosis. However free-form he may be in
the beginning, by the time he invades France in the last play of
the trilogy, Hal has become as cold and self-contained as the
figure Freud describes. Hal banishes Falstaff, who has taught
him so much, and he hangs his old drinking buddy, Bardolph.
By the end of the play, Hal, a little like Michael Corleone at
the end of Francis Ford Coppola's masterpiece, *The Godfather
Part II*, truly loves no one but himself. Despite some subdued
ironies directed against the king in *Henry V*, the play suggests
that, as humanly off-putting as the self-loving Hal may be, he
is nonetheless a superbly effective monarch. For the people
need such rulers. With kings who can also jest, who can take
themselves lightly, if only at times, they can have nothing
serious to do. Such figures do not command allegiance.
Falstaffian figures cannot activate the fantasies of omnipotence that we all, Freud argues, attached to our fathers when

we were children, and that we still nurse in the unconscious. Northrop Frye observes that men will die for a brutal autocrat, but not for a joking backslapper. Freud, and Shakespeare as well, can offer reasons why this might be so.

Freud believed that in reading the book of Shakespeare, he read the book of nature. Even if he did not draw his theory of the leader directly from Shakespeare's pages, he could at least have found it corroborated here. In fact, Freud's vision of the leader and Shakespeare's are barely distinguishable, except that Freud is rather disgusted by the human weakness the vision reveals, and Shakespeare seems to see Hal's sort of kingship as simply necessary.

From *Hamlet*, Freud draws much of the material he needed to formulate the Oedipus complex. He does so directly. But all through Freud there are instances of convergence with Shakespeare. What these instances indicate, at least to me, is that Freud effectively acts as a literary critic of Shakespeare. He takes the work at hand and draws a theory of human nature and of human social life from it. Freud has seen that Shakespeare poses the question "What is life?" and he has done his best to construe his answer.

And this, in fact, is what literary criticism ought to do. A valuable literary critic is not someone who debunks canonical figures, or who puts writers into their historical contexts, or, in general, one who propounds new and brilliant theories of interpretation. A valuable critic, rather, is one who brings forth the philosophy of life latent in major works of art and imagination. He makes the author's implicit wisdom explicit, and he offers that wisdom to the judgment of the world.

When he encounters works that are not wise but foolish, what he does, in general, is to leave them alone—he doesn't teach them, or write about them, or give them any more notice than they already have. The world is aflood with bad ideas and flawed visions: the true critic seeks and finds live options; he heralds forgotten news that is still new. He discovers the discoveries of art.

The truest example of literary criticism I know of is this one: one July day in 1855, Ralph Waldo Emerson, by far the preeminent man of letters in America, received by post a volume of poetry from an absolutely unknown carpenter living in Brooklyn, New York. The volume had been privately printed, since no commercial publisher would touch it. Its author sold it door to door; he also reviewed it himself, anonymously: "An American bard at last," one of the reviews began. Emerson, who in himself concentrated the prestige of all of our current literary Nobel Prize winners rolled into one, did not do what one might expect. He did not take the volume and toss it into the trash.

He took it into his home, read it, and immediately, with a shock of recognition, felt its genius. He called it the greatest piece of wit and wisdom that America had yet produced. He overwhelmed the unknown author with praise. He endorsed the book to everyone he knew.

Emerson himself had always hoped to matter preeminently as a poet. In his essay on the uses of poets and poetry, he described the kind of writer he thought America most needed and that he himself aspired to be, someone responsive to the variety, energy, and promise of the new nation: "Our logrolling, our stumps and their politics, our fisheries, our Negroes, and Indians, our boasts, and our repudiations, the wrath of rogues, and the pusillanimity of honest men, the northern trade, the southern planting, the western clearing, Oregon, and Texas, are yet unsung. Yet America is a poem in our eyes; its ample geography dazzles the imagination, and it will not wait long for metres." It was clear to Emerson that, much as he wanted to fill that role, he never would. He was a poet of the inner self, not of teeming democracy. But when he saw someone else rise to the task, he didn't turn away with resentment, or offer measured, feline praise. When Walt Whitman sent Emerson the first volume of *Leaves of Grass*, Emerson forgot himself and embraced a new hero.

Hamlet

POETRY, HORACE SAID, ought to give pleasure and instruct. And one need not look only to Freud to find instruction in the work of Shakespeare. There are other ways to go.

The Romantics took Hamlet as the representative contemporary individual, and their instinct was in many ways just. Hamlet stands between the Homeric figure that Bowra describes and the Christian ethos. He feels impelled by his father's ghost to take revenge and murder King Claudius. Hamlet the Elder is a figure steeped in the old heroic code. He would have looked to Achilles as an exemplar. When someone kills a member of your clan, you don't turn the other cheek, or even call on God to deliver just punishment. You strike, in as quick and deadly a way as you can.

Hamlet is responsive to this warrior code. Yet at the same time, he feels constrained by a Christian sense of right and wrong. *Thou shalt not kill.* Thou shalt not take revenge. Hamlet is a thinker, a deeply inward man with a Christian conscience. But along with that conscience he possesses the residue of a Homeric drive for ascendancy. He wants preeminence.

The tension between these two ways of life, Christian and Homeric, informs the language of the play, the language that

Hamlet himself speaks. No interpretation of the play is complete without a careful study of the protagonist's idiom. But such responsiveness is only part of a full reaction to the play. At the beginning of his first solioquy, Hamlet makes his Christian commitment clear, calling out "God, God," and wishing that "the Everlasting had not fix'd / His canon 'gainst self-slaughter." Suicide can, of course, be a noble end in the classical world. In Christianity it is entirely forbidden.

Not much later, Hamlet moves from the idiom of Christianity to the idiom of classical antiquity. His dead father is "Hyperion," his usurping uncle a "satyr." Then his mother is weeping Niobe. He cries out against Gertrude for marrying his uncle—"my father's brother, but no more like my father / Than I to Hercules." In part, Hamlet wishes he could be Hercules, the better to rise to his father's revenge. But to his Christian conscience, Hercules is a throwback, a barbarian ideal.

Paul Cantor, the source of this Nietzschean reading of *Hamlet,* summarizes the situation: "In some ways, the figure of the ghost encapsulates the polarities Hamlet faces. As the ghost of his *father,* dressed in military garb and crying for revenge, it conjures up the world of epic warfare and heroic combat. But as the *ghost* of his father, rising out of what appears to be purgatory, it shatters the narrow bounds of the pagan imagination and opens a window on the eternal vistas of Christianity. In short, the ghost is at one and the same time a pagan and a Christian figure, and as such points to the heart of Hamlet's tragic dilemma as a modern Christian charged with the ancient pagan task of revenge."

Hamlet is caught between two worldviews, two circles or narratives—a state that may be the essential condition of tragedy. He is looking toward both Jesus and Achilles, two dutiful sons whose piety is in dramatic opposition, to see which way he needs to go.

The result is delay, irresolution. But, we must ask—and our students with us—is Hamlet's lot not sometimes ours, too? Many of the crises that give us the greatest pain and that are, in their effects on our day-to-day lives, potentially tragic, involve the collision of these two sets of values, Christian and pagan. Are we for or against capital punishment? Shall we follow the old classical code of honor or the modern code of mercy when a fellow citizen has been wronged? And abortion? Shall we do as the classical world did and, without excessive qualms, snuff out the newborn or unborn for our own advantage, or even our own convenience? Or shall we go the way of the Gospels and be, like Jesus, shepherds of souls? (Not some souls, but all of them.) Contemplating suicide, some of our contemporaries will also inevitably hear voices contending in a way that evokes Hamlet. To the classical world, as Shakespeare accurately dramatizes it in *Julius Caesar,* suicide can be an honorable end. It offers a dignified exit from a life that would otherwise end in shame. To the Christian mind, suicide is associated with acedia, or despair, the crime against the Holy Spirit, and the one unforgivable sin.

When these two worldviews, Christian and classical, enter conflict, it is unlikely that we will be able to find a satisfying compromise. Hegel believed that tragedy began when two highly desirable and mutually exclusive courses of action collided with each other. For Hegel, tragedy is two rights making a wrong. Two rights make a wrong for Hamlet, and often, I suspect, for us as well, as we confront prospects for action—revenge, suicide, abortion—that dramatically divide our spirits. Encounters of this sort will not offer satisfying resolutions. There is not likely to be any plan of action that can leave us fully at peace. And frequently, the result will be grief of tragic proportions.

Not every interpretation geared to discovering usable truths leads us to happiness. Not every such reading answers questions. Tragic awareness, which Shakespeare often bequeaths, can only reveal to us that certain griefs are not fully negotiable, cannot be readily converted into happiness or tranquillity. (Robert Frost thought that a central element of a literary education was learning to distinguish grief from grievances. Grievances may be remediable; griefs are to be suffered.) But perhaps in the foreknowledge of such sorrows there is some consolation; at least one will not be taken entirely by surprise.

Good Medicine?

IS THE KIND of literary education that I'm endorsing here a form of therapy? Yes and no. Yes, in that this kind of teaching, like Socrates', like Freud's, offers possibilities for change that are not only intellectual but also emotional. When we're talking about Final Narratives, we're talking about ultimate values, and strong feelings inevitably come out; tensions similar to the ones that proliferate in Freudian analysis can arise. (I sometimes preside over a raucous classroom.) But there is also a crucial difference. Patients come to psychoanalysis because they suffer from the past. Their obsessions, in some measure unconscious, with past events prevent their living with reasonable fullness in the present. The form of teaching that I espouse assumes a certain ability to live now (that is to say, a certain sanity) and so aims itself not primarily at unearthing the past, but at shaping the future. What will you be? What will you do?

There is a story about a psychoanalyst who, after the first day's intake interview, asked his patients an unexpected question. "If you were cured right now, if you were well, what would you do?" There would usually come forth a list. "I'd get married; I'd travel; I'd go back to school and study law." To which the therapist, trusting his instincts, sometimes replied, "Then why don't you go off and do those things?" Assuming that he posed that question at the right moment, to the right patient, then what the analyst had observed was that the analysand was not caught in the past, but was actually alive enough to the promise of futurity (healthy enough) to expand out of his existing sphere.

In a marvelous passage in his book on Freud, the philosopher Paul Ricoeur describes the moment when the Oedipus complex stops being a regressive trap for the individual and begins to be a sign of future promise, a provocation to do some fresh work in the world. This is the moment when the father is no longer the mystical foe, but an ambivalent ally whose own contributions to the world one can, however subtly, however strongly, revise. The person who stands on the edge, between regression and progress, past and future, is the one who has made herself ripe for literary education.

So the approach to teaching the humanities I am describing is not therapeutic per se. Nor, as I hope the discussion of Hamlet shows, is it to be written off as a way of dispensing elevating platitudes. It's not an exercise in cheering yourself up. Teachers should feel free to introduce the most appalling visions to their students. To read the Marquis de Sade, with his insistence that sexualized cruelty is the deepest desire of all men and women, is to encounter a way of apprehending life that can qualify as a vital option, if only to some. The objective of this kind of teaching is not to pretend that the Marquis does not exist, or that the disgustingly anti-Semitic Celine is not a writer worth serious study, or that Pound's fascism puts him out of bounds. Rather, it is to encounter such works and put them to the test of imagined experience. What would it be like to go Sade's way? What is to be gained and what lost in the life of the libertine?

It is not the professor's business to eradicate every form of what he takes to be retrograde and disgusting behavior. All student perspectives are welcome in class; whether they are racist, or homophobic, or whatever, they must be heard, considered, and responded to without panic. The classroom I am describing is a free space, one where people can speak their innermost thoughts and bring what is dark to light. They may expect to be challenged, but not to be shouted down, written off, or ostracized. Bitter, brutal thoughts can grow prolifically in the mind's unlighted cellars. But when we bring them into the world and examine them dispassionately, they often lose their force.

A few sessions into studying Orwell's *Nineteen Eighty-Four*, I asked a question that touched on the students' sense of self. "If you woke up tomorrow in Orwell's world, what path would you take? Would you try to blend in, as most people do? Or would you resist, in Winston Smith's way, defending truth as you perceived it, against all the surrounding lies? Or would you go Julia's route and live for pleasure in the midst of an insanely puritanical world?" (Julia, it's said, is a "rebel from the waist down.") The first answer I got shocked me. "I'd be O'Brien," a young woman said. O'Brien may be the most memorable character in the book: he's a gifted intellectual and high functionary of the inner party, who has become a horrible sadist. He takes a nearly sexual delight in reducing Smith from a resister to a cringing lump. "I'd try to put myself on the top, just like I try to now," Elizabeth went on. "And I think a lot of people here would do the same thing." As soon as Elizabeth said as much, we weren't having an ordinary conversation anymore, but a dialogue about the way we ought to live our lives.

A good classroom is a free-speech zone, where everything can be expressed, and where, at times, one will read authors who are not, in the teacher's opinion, conducive to a form of the good life, but are prophets of cruelty and hatred. We will explore their visions. We will bring to the fore the experimental selves they provide, and ask ourselves: what would it mean to live like that?

Most of the books we teach, especially to the young, will contain, implicitly or overtly, versions of the good life that we can endorse. But not all. We will, I hope, have faith that, given fair hearing, those imaginative voices that lead to health, generosity, energy, humor, and compassion will win out over the other sort. But we will also know that such a victory is not foreordained.

Not long ago I met a very likable and generous professor of humanities. He was mild-mannered, but no pushover. What he had to say about his own way of teaching fascinated me.

"It seems to me," he said, "that every generation of humanities teachers has worked, subtly and quietly, to make students into more progressive people. We've encouraged them to be skeptical about religious belief. We've helped them to be more open-minded in their response to others, particularly when they're different. And we've particularly worked to persuade the guys that their masculinity won't be lost if they become more sensitive than they were before. We've tried to suggest that a no-holds-barred capitalism isn't the best thing for everyone and we've tried to push in the direction of more and more social and economic equality. We've tried to change the way people get pleasure out of life. We've shown them that there's more than TV; they can enjoy poetry and opera and philosophy. You can probably say that we've tried to make them more civilized."

I found this well put and plausible. Maybe America would be

a better place if this professor's educational goals came to fruition. It would be a more humane country if we all became more sensitive, more community minded, less materialistic, more civilized.

"So," I said, "it's as though what you're trying to do is make them into honorary Europeans, postmodern, postreligious citizens of Paris or Brussels?"

He agreed. That was exactly what he was shooting for. But thinking further on the matter, it strikes me that it's a very bad idea for us teachers to have a preexisting image of how we want our students to turn out, even as potentially attractive an idea as this teacher was offering. No, I think that what we need is for people to understand who and what they are now, then to be open to changing into their own highest mode of being. And that highest mode is something that they must identify by themselves, through encounters with the best that has been known and thought. We all have promise in us; it is up to education to reveal that promise, and to help it unfold. The power that is in you, says Emerson, is new in nature. And the best way to release that power is to let students confront viable versions of experience and take their choices.

It will come as little surprise when I say that what I have been endorsing here is a form of humanism. Humanism has a long and complex history, but for the purposes of this book, I want to describe humanistic education in a relatively condensed way. To me, humanism is the belief that it is possible for some of us, and maybe more than some, to use secular writing as the preeminent means for shaping our lives. That means that we might construct ourselves from novels, poems, and plays, as well as from works of history and philosophy, in the way that our ancestors constructed themselves (and were constructed) by the Bible and other sacred texts.

To me, the drawback of significant past versions of humanism is that they have all come with latent and overt ideas about the person they wanted to see emerge from the process of reading and thinking. Like my friend the kindly professor, humanists have known from the start what sort of person they hoped to create. The New Critics, with their emphasis on those qualities— a capacity for irony and ambiguity, the power to maintain inner tension—that they saw as conducive to maturity, did precisely this, encouraging their devotees to be responsive to a preexisting model. Matthew Arnold, who usefully announced to the world that in the time to come poetry might have to replace religion as the source of spiritual sustenance, was himself narrowly committed. Arnold gave us the touchstones, passages at the heart of true literature, passages that all of us needed to grapple to our souls so as to become genuinely educated. But Arnold's stoical resignation, the discourse of tempered middle age, will not do for everyone.

Later on, Jacques Derrida undermined Jean-Paul Sartre's humanism by pointing out the metaphysical, which is to say the subtly coercive, base on which it rests. Asked to provide a standard that could guide the individual in his choice of actions—with action understood to be at the core of the existentialist's philosophy of life—Sartre makes the mistake of responding in a generalizing and delimiting way: Act always in such a manner that you are working to create a self that could serve as a model for others. We are back with Kant, back under the shadow of the categorical imperative, and back to a coercive form of pedagogy that is not at all consistent with hopes for self-reliant freedom. Even Heidegger, who in the "Letter on Humanism" tries to distance himself from Sartre, is accurately criticized by Derrida for propounding a kind of philosophical monotheism. Derrida sees that Heidegger himself has a preordained ideal to which all human development should aspire. Heidegger celebrates something called Being and, more precisely, the individual's apprehension of and identification with a pure state of existence. For Heidegger, the highest human destiny is to be the "shepherd of Being." Yet Derrida himself, as shrewdly as he may write in "The Ends of Man," has nothing of a positive nature to offer. He has no vision of possible human development. Derrida limits himself to the work of clearing away superannuated and delimiting modes of humanistic thinking, and then can do no more.

T. S. Eliot, in the great essay "Tradition and the Individual Talent," tried to found a humanism by positing the existence of literary monuments that could be modified by the intervention of this or that newly canonical writer. Encountering Eliot on the canon, I think of Kierkegaard, who said of Hegel that the *Phenomenology* would rank as one of the greatest of all works if only its author had the sense to finish by saying that it was merely a thought experiment, only one idiosyncratic version of the way that it all is. One might say something similar of Eliot. If only the monuments were explicitly and joyously *his* monuments, his and no one else's. If only he told us all to go out and make, from the profusion of magnificent works that surround us, something on the order of a quotidian liturgy, a secular scripture, as Frye liked to call it, of our own. "I must Create a System," as Blake, Frye's great teacher, put it, "or be enslav'd by another Mans." Eliot, the potential liberator, becomes a creator of what Blake, hyperbolist that he sometimes was, called "mindforg'd manacles." Even Frye, author of the greatest book of visionary literary criticism yet written—for it takes visionary powers to make a past writer's vision live in the present— eventually throws his wonderful energy and intelligence into forming a system. The master system of *Anatomy of Criticism* reveals all of literature's meanings; in it all readers should believe. But such systems pass quickly away. They will always be replaced by other coercive and exclusionary intellectual organizations that offer the comforts of collective, institutional religion—at least, until we can discover what Blake knew: that all deities ultimately reside in the individual human breast.

Disciples

IT IS SOMETIMES hard for us critics to see that we are disciples. Or that we ought to be. The fact does not sort well with our dignity. But in fact the true T. S. Eliot scholar is not a grubber after Eliot-related facts, or the creator of ingeniously baroque readings of Eliot. He is not the source of minutiae for the Eliot newsletter or any other such thing. No, he is far more important than that, and also far less.

He is, or ought to be, Eliot's disciple. He is responsible for so immersing himself in Eliot that only he and very few others can plausibly bring Eliot's vision alive in the current world, which, as the critic deeply believes (or why would he have become a deep student of Eliot to begin with?), has sore need of it. He is the one who will know instinctively—as Frye knew of Blake, as Bate knew of Keats and Johnson, as Orwell knew of Dickens— precisely how his author would feel in response to virtually any event that comes to pass around us.

We fancy we are saying something merely rhetorical when we talk about how authors who matter live on forever. But it is not figurative speech at all, if a literary culture is unfolding as it should. No, the scholar by dint of hard work and imagination can, at will, merge himself with the authors who matter to him. By the exercise of his own heart's intelligence, he manages to keep them alive in the present. By sacrificing some of his individuality to the thoughts and feelings of another, by giving up himself, he becomes a light of knowledge to all around him. And when the scholar does not do so, our common culture suffers.

When I was in graduate school, I became a student of Freud. It seemed necessary then to learn absolutely everything I could about him. I read his works numberless times; I read everything about him that I could get. And his vision fully infiltrated my mind. On any given subject, then and now, I can offer a plausible Freudian response, though by this time I believe at best a significant fraction of what Freud did. This kind of study involves a certain self-annulling, not unrelated to the annulment of self that Eliot describes in "Tradition and the Individual Talent." There, Eliot speaks of the poet's surrender of personality in order to make way for the influence of past poets. "What happens is a continual surrender of himself as he is at the moment to something which is more valuable." Such learning—and I don't mean to single myself out here; many people have it—is part of what a scholar's education is about. My job as a Romanticist is not primarily to say unprecedented things about the Romantics, or to go to conferences and impress my fellow scholars, most of whom actively dislike the authors they teach, anyway. My job is to continue the lives of the poets on in the present, to make them available to those living now who might need them.

It's not necessary to be a lifelong scholar of this or that writer to make his work available to the uses of the present and future. Learning surely helps a great deal, but energy, imagination, and a little judiciousness go a long way, too. What's most important, I think, is to find the writer at the peak of his potential for life. You can dwell on Dostoyevsky as the writer who conveys an astounding and just portrait of a certain sort of murderer in *Crime and Punishment*. But ultimately, one probably does more for students by helping them to understand Dostoyevsky's vision of life as an insane, ever-blackening turbulence that we can only navigate humanely by recourse to religious faith.

A given age is likely to be infused to the core with standard prevailing opinion, which is the product of the moment. The day is generally suffused with—recall William Carlos Williams's lines—"what passes for the new." One way to break through that prevailing opinion is to have recourse to the best that has been known and thought in the past. Offering past wealth to the present is what a scholar is supposed to do.

Sometimes someone steps from our ranks whose own vision of matters is worthy of consideration in its own right. But most of us cannot lay fair claim to that power. Rather, we are the powers that keep Chaucer and Spenser and Milton from fading into oblivion. This is a noble task. And rightly universities give people security, relative calm, and a solid sustenance to let it unfold.

Are you so original? Such an adept translator or rewriter of texts? Come out from behind the pretense. Write us your own novel or poem or essay, take up matters where there is more pressure on the individual to compound his way of apprehending things, and let us see what you have on offer. Then we may judge whether you might not have been better off with the genuinely noble, if also more modest, process of discipleship. And if you stay with true discipleship, who knows? Does Plato not go at least as far as Socrates? Does Frye at his best not do more than complete Blake? Such achievement must come naturally, through a process that begins in some measure of self-annulment. Yet it is a self-annulment that can be amply rewarded. As Camille Paglia puts it, "Great teachers live their subject. The subject teaches itself through them. It uses them and, in return, charges them with elemental energy."

Exemplars

THE KIND OF teaching I endorse entails impersonation. The teacher temporarily becomes the author, valuing what the author values, thinking as the author would. George Orwell does this for Dickens in his wonderful essay on the novelist. Marilyn Butler does it for Jane Austen; Harold Bloom for Wallace Stevens; Geoffrey Hartman and Walter Jackson Bate for Keats. Helen Vendler has done it for many contemporary poets in her review-essays. With unparalleled brilliance, Northrop Frye does it in his book on William Blake, *Fearful Symmetry*. These critics merge with their authors and by doing so become more than who they are.

Such critics are not only valuable in themselves, but valuable in dialogue with one another. Consider what is to be gained by juxtaposing Butler and Frye on the subject of the Romantics. For years, Frye immersed himself in Blake's work; he thought and probably even dreamed as Blake would. And the result is a remarkable transfiguration. Frye becomes Blake, or at least a highly plausible version of Blake. It is a Blake who is alive to the needs of Frye's present, an available, cogent Blake who speaks to Frye's society and, I believe, to our own.

Listen to Frye, in one of many memorable passages, matching the eloquence of Blake to bring him to us. "Inspiration," writes Blake-Frye, "is the artist's empirical proof of the divinity of his imagination; and all inspiration is divine in origin, whether used, perverted, hidden or frittered away in reverie. All imaginative and creative acts, being eternal, go to build up a permanent structure, which Blake calls Golgonooza, above time, and, when this structure is finished, nature, its scaffolding, will be knocked away and man will live in it. Golgonooza will then be the city of God, the new Jerusalem which is the total form of all human culture and civilization. Nothing that the heroes, martyrs, prophets and poets of the past have done for it has been wasted; no anonymous and unrecognized contribution to it has been overlooked. In it is conserved all the good man has done, and in it is completed all that he hoped and intended to do. And the artist who uses the same energy and genius that Homer and Isaiah had will find that he not only lives in the same palace of art as Homer and Isaiah, but lives in it at the same time."

This is Frye's version of Eliot's "Tradition and the Individual Talent." For Eliot, most of us must live outside the world of great works, looking on in awe. But Frye's imaginative world is a world for you and for me, a democratic world of art and creation that we can enter by making an honest attempt to write with visionary integrity. We need to render what we see as truly as we can. In so doing we can come into the world of genius—feeling, perhaps, the shock of recognition that Melville said united all who deployed the energies of creation, whether they succeeded in worldly terms or failed. (Melville put his own relation to worldly success memorably: "So far as I am individually concerned, & independent of my pocket, it is my earnest desire to write those sort of books which are said to 'fail.'")

What Frye offers, through reliance on the self, is entry into Keats's immortal freemasonry of intellect. The aim of a liberal arts education, from this perspective, is to show us that, as Walter Jackson Bate puts it, "we need not be the passive victims of what we deterministically call 'circumstances' (social, cultural, or reductively psychological-personal), but that by linking ourselves through what Keats calls an 'immortal free-masonry' with the great we can become freer—freer to be ourselves, to be what we most want and value."

Frye imagines opening the world of artistic freedom to ever growing numbers of people; he is self-consciously democratizing where Eliot is exclusionary. But the energies of art do not belong to everyone simply by virtue of being born. One has to strive to enter into the world of Homer and Isaiah and to draw on their powers. The most admirable individuals, for Frye and Blake, will be the ones who throw themselves into the life of creation; those who refuse the opportunity have turned away from what matters most in life. "The worship of God," wrote Blake, "is Honouring his gifts in other men each according to his genius and loving the greatest men best."

As arresting as this affirmation of genius may be, it probably should not go without challenge in a classroom. For perhaps there are other paths, and before the student is swept in by the attractions of Blake and Frye, and Keats and Bate, it's necessary to look critically at them.

Taking a deep initial delight in a book or an author is a little like falling in love. There is a nearly rapturous acceptance of all the author brings. The truth unfolds as if from above. But to adapt that vision to one's own uses, to bring it wisely into the world, more than love is necessary. One also has to apply a critical scrutiny to the work—consider its connotations, examine its antecedents, asking always: What would it mean to live this vision? The initial feeling of being swept off your feet by a book has got to be followed by more thoughtful commitment, as marriage follows love. When you say yes to an author's vision, you're entering into a marriage of minds. And such marriage ought not to take place without critical scrutiny.

In *Romantics, Rebels and Reactionaries*, Marilyn Butler is generally about as detached from her subject as Frye is immersed in his. But at one point, she steps forward and affirms her identification with Jane Austen, using Austen to contend against the self-generated visions that the Romantics and their proponents worship. Here is Butler: "In all Jane Austen's novels, characters are judged by their manners. But one is not born with manners, nor can one easily pick them up; one is taught them as a child by parents who had them. The issue of manners is raised more explicitly in German literature of Jane Austen's period than in English. In that country of legalized class distinctions, burger writers could not rise socially; they had to use their inner resources, and make a self-justifying system out of solipsism—Romanticism is such a system—because their manners, or lack of them, would always exclude them from the charmed circle of the hereditary aristocracy. For Jane Austen, the writer who expresses the ethos of the landed gentry, manners are indeed the passport. But true to her function at its highest, she idealizes manners and endows them with all their theoretical value . . . They proclaim that the old style of social responsibility is accepted, *duty* (the idealized reading of upper-class motivation) put before the new individualism."

Blake and Frye are avatars of Romantic individualism, and they are, to Butler, an error that must be attacked, both in the past and present; to her, they make a system out of an aggressive, resentful solipsism. For Butler, Romanticism is a plague, something that tears society apart, encouraging us to live only for ourselves. It must be shown up for what it is. Greatly preferring Blake-Frye as I do, full of gratitude to Frye for performing the task Schopenhauer sets out and making Blake's work unfold as a contemporary answer to the question "What is life?," I find little to agree with in Butler. But in teaching Austen alongside Blake, as I often do, Butler seems to me key in helping students to see the differences between the two and to begin to make some choices, choices that will matter not just in class but for future life.

Of course Blake does want us *all* to live in Golgonooza, the city of ongoing creation, but you get there by being an inspired artist, by trusting yourself and by being yourself with the greatest possible gusto. And this is not something that everyone is prone to do. As Oscar Wilde put it, "Most people are other people."

What matters about these critics is that they are writing accurately about their authors (at least insofar as I can see) and doing so with *the conduct of life* as their concern. They are asking what it means to live the authors at hand. They are mining them for vital options, questing for truth.

Orwell's Dickens

GEORGE ORWELL'S ESSAY on Charles Dickens is not an academic investigation, a fresh interpretation from the standpoint of Marx or Freud or whomever else you might care to apply for the purposes of translation. Rather, the piece is an internal argument—it's Orwell contending with himself. He is pitting what I take to be his own early infatuation with Dickens against what he has learned later in life through his immersion in politics (and war) as well as through his study of Marx and other social thinkers. Orwell seems to be writing this essay because he needs to. He needs—while describing Dickens with all the accuracy he can muster—to find out whether he, and by extension his readers, ought to take to heart the truth in Dickens's work.

Dickens, as Orwell has come in time to see, has no social doctrine. Perhaps he is unmatched at dramatizing injustice but, to Orwell, Dickens has no conception of how various social arrangements conspire to create it. When Dickens wants to indict evil, or inhumanity, he indicts this or that inhumane person or inhumane act. His scope is entirely limited to what he can see in front of him. Dickens has no capacity to step back and to envision things in their larger, more general workings. "He has no constructive suggestions," Orwell says, "not even a clear grasp of the nature of the society he is attacking, only an emotional perception that something is wrong."

A case in point, for Orwell, is Dickens's view of education: "He attacks the current educational system with perfect justice, and yet, after all, he has no remedy to offer except kindlier schoolmasters. Why did he not indicate what a school *might* have been? Why did he not have his own sons educated according to some plan of his own, instead of sending them to public school to be stuffed with Greek? Because he lacked that kind of imagination."

"He lacked that kind of imagination": by which Orwell means that he lacked a political imagination. Theories of education, as Plato demonstrates in *The Republic*, are always political theories, blueprints for future societies. Dickens had no political theory. He was unable to conceive of an alternative to the slash-and-burn capitalism that was developing everywhere around him. He could protest against institutions, but he could not imagine their replacement with better ones. Rather, the man behind the functionary's desk must become a better man. Orwell, it's soon clear, is arguing with himself, for and against socialism, the doctrine that Dickens could have adopted and never did, and the doctrine that is tempting Orwell himself. When Orwell chides Dickens, early on in the essay, for not having a social imagination, what he means is that he has no imagination for socialism.

Orwell's argument with himself, and with his own prior love

for Dickens, is so honest, nondogmatic, and uncommitted to preordained conclusions, that by the close of the essay he has, it seems, discovered something. The process of writing the essay appears to have remade his mind. Yeats said that when you have an argument with the world, you write an essay. When the argument is with yourself, it issues in a poem. This is an argument with the self that results in an essay replete with the passion that comes in the best poems.

Here is Orwell on the limits of the kind of socialist thought that he has been measuring Dickens against. "All [Dickens] can finally say is 'Behave decently,' which . . . is not necessarily so shallow as it sounds. Most revolutionaries are potential Tories, because they imagine that everything can be put right by altering the *shape* of society; once that change is effected, as it sometimes is, they see no need for any other. Dickens has not this kind of mental coarseness. The vagueness of his discontent is the mark of its permanence. What he is out against is not this or that institution, but, as Chesterton put it, 'an expression on the human face.'" In fact, Orwell now sees, Dickens's permanent radicalism may well be more attractive than the temporary discontent, aimed at the overthrow of an existing system, that so-called revolutionaries maintain. The revolutionaries want to replace the current system with another that will last for all time—the dictatorship of the proletariat, maybe—and that will almost inevitably solidify and hem in life.

Orwell in his youth seems to have fallen in love with Dickens. And the first phase in being influenced by a writer—influenced in the best sense—is precisely such love. But the process must go further than that. To actually adopt a writer's vision, the reader has to engage in critical examination. The writer needs to answer the hardest questions one can put to him, because, in effect, these are our questions, our perplexities about how to live and what to do. Just so, when we are on the verge of marriage, we need to know that love is at the core of it all. But we also need to think hard about our choice. What kind of mother or father will the person make? Will she bear with me in bad times as well as good, sickness as well as health, poverty and wealth alike? Posing such questions of an author's vision—can it sustain me in the hard hours as well as the sweet?—is central to the act of criticism that precedes consequential belief.

Some students will go even further. So far, we have been talking about two sorts of people: those who are reasonably comfortable with the values they've been socialized to accept, and those who feel an uneasiness with them, however latent. This second group is ripe for literary study. They need a second chance to come of age. But some of them will not be satisfied with what they find in books, however much it may draw them. They'll see that Shelley or Austen goes only so far, and they'll feel the need to complete and correct the writers they love by writing novels and poems and essays of their own. Writers become writers for many reasons, but one is that the books on the shelf are never quite the right books. They don't render the world in exactly the way that it is. So there is reason to write more. Walter Benjamin tells the story of a village schoolmaster who was too poor to buy books; when he saw a title in a catalog that intrigued him, he sat down and composed the volume himself. "Writers," Benjamin observes, "are really people who write books not because they are poor, but because they are dissatisfied with the books which they could buy but do not like."

Influence

WHEN SOME TEACHERS think about this approach to education, they find the issue of influence particularly troubling. They are concerned that they might become propagandists, rather than what they hope to be, critical thinkers who enjoin critical thought. They don't want to implant ways of seeing things in their students, using their authority and the powers of their grades. Rather, they want to echo the advice that Johnson gave Boswell, turn to their students and demand that they rid their minds of cant. What is to be put in the place of this cant— or doxa, or ideology, or, if you like, bullshit—the critical thinkers rarely say.

To me, there are few pleasures greater than being influenced: learning something I need to know from another. Longinus describes this feeling of connection with a great author in a splendid sentence when he says that when we encounter sublime wisdom, we feel that we have created what in fact we've only heard. The utterance so much echoes our latent wisdom that we take the author's words as our own. Emerson, greatly fearing influence, especially early in his career, speaks of the indignity of being "forced to take with shame our own opinion from another." But Emerson addresses us here as an aspiring original. To the true reader, every form of usable truth is welcome many times over. Later in life, Emerson is more circumspect: "Shall I tell you the secret of the true scholar? It is this: Every man I meet is my master in some point, and in that I learn of him."

Many of our students have grown up being suffused with TV, movies, video games. Is what is to be found in Blake and Dickens so much worse than what Paramount and Disney have to deliver? Should we suffer endless qualms lest the world according to Spielberg be displaced by the world according to Wallace Stevens? Yet there is something real about these concerns; teaching in the way that I describe does have its dangers.

To me, part of the risk of true teaching lies in the willingness to see students make choices, sometimes bad choices. We must not be afraid of submitting our students to influence. We face people who are on the verge of major decisions. Should I marry? Should I have children? Should I go into law? Should I stay in my parents' church? Such questions matter to young people, and they matter now. If thinking about these questions in a classroom can be dangerous, it can be much more dangerous not to think about them. The result of never brooding over major issues is likely to be that one follows the crowd. One takes common convention as a guide. Rich in use as convention can be, for some it is stifling, begetting lives of quiet desperation. We spend our days pursuing ends that outrage our natures, making ourselves sick, as Thoreau said, so that we can lay something up against our coming illness. A fundamental qualification for teaching literature should be the view that great books are worth studying, and because of the salutary effects that they can have on life. Why would a student wish to study with anyone who didn't think as much? Doing so would be like hiring a lawyer who had lost all of his faith in the law and didn't want to sully himself through contact with the corrupt legal system.

The professors who become most uneasy about asking their students real questions are often those with the most doubts about the capacities of everyday people to make their own decisions and to direct their own lives. These professors, whatever they may say, are fundamentally afraid of living in a democracy, where people think for themselves, rather than letting experts do their thinking for them. This fear is a scandal at the center of the current day academy. Though many professors claim to be on the left, the fact is that they do not trust, or sometimes even much like, everyday, relatively unschooled people. In fact, they tend to despise the people in whose behalf they claim to be working.

As disconcerting to me as the fears of those who think that students will be too easily swayed are the doubts of those who feel that human beings can be changed little, if at all, for the better. Eminent among these is Sigmund Freud. What Freud calls the transference is purportedly an inescapable part of life, perhaps even an element of every significant encounter. The theory of the transference suggests that we live eternally in the past, never in the present and future. To Freud, we perpetually approach figures of authority and figures of erotic interest not as the people they are in themselves, but rather as though they were figures from our past. The boss's injunctions are inflected with the mother's commands. The lover's carpings are the father's as well. We are lost in a world where, as J. H. van den Berg puts it, "everything is past and there is nothing new." We find ourselves amidst facsimiles of replicas of reproductions.

One of the reasons that Freud hated America as much as he did is that the nation seemed organized on the premise that the present could have a liberated relation to the past. We believed that it was possible to draw on the past, not be swallowed by it against our wills. Democracy, which depends on the enfranchisement of greater and greater numbers of people, on the widening of their possibilities, is inseparable from faith in the present and future.

To have gone into teaching is to have placed one's wager on the hopeful side of the question. By choosing to teach, we have declared a hope that the powers of nurture may be a little stronger than nature's. We've affirmed the hope that the present can be more alive than the constricting past. What is our proof beyond that hope? Do we have any evidence, besides our temperamental wish to think well of the world? I think so. As teachers we see proof all the time. We see proof, first of all, in the nearly miraculous works that we often teach. If a human being can write as Shakespeare or Blake did, coming from humble beginnings, with no advantages other than those they created themselves, then what is not to be hoped for from an individual man or woman? "A human being did that!" one says, reading their work. "And what might I, too, no less human, be able to achieve?"

Freud and all the other purveyors of the Gothic imagination may be right. It's possible that the present is bound so tightly to the past that it rarely breaks free. Edgar Allan Poe, the ultimate Gothic writer, delighted in depicting people who are fated from the start to be devoured by past sins, whether they committed them or not. Is there any doubt, once you see the enormous crack running through the House of Usher, what will happen to it and its residents by the tale's end? Poe, who sought his own doom ruthlessly enough, seemed to believe that all of us would eventually be sacrificed on the altar of long-ago transgressions.

Education is a gamble. Socrates was gambling when he asked his young friends to put their beliefs into play. Jesus was gambling when he told streetcorner denizens, in whose eyes he saw something unsatisfied, to get up and follow him, put aside the begging bowl or the tax collectors' book. The Buddha gambled when he told people that they could free themselves from the wheel of incarnation through meditation and awareness of the noble truths. This is what teachers, great and small, do: they wager that they can help people become one with their highest promise. Freud once said that the aim of therapy was to turn misery into common everyday unhappiness—and one admires the tough-mindedness in his remark. But Thoreau, himself an estimable figure, talked about bringing the past into the thousand-eyed light of the present, and living forever in a new day. And from what I can tell from *Walden*'s best pages, sometimes he did.

Thoreau and Emerson do not wish to throw out the past. Emerson, for his part, wrote a book on representative individuals, historical figures from whom we might learn. And Whitman said, in his preface to *Leaves of Grass*, that America does not repudiate what is done and gone. Rather, we draw on it for fresh life, ingest it and make it new, as the body does its food. If you've become a teacher, you've already entered the game on the Emersonian side; you're there to change people, help them live better. The scholar Andrew Delbanco quotes Emerson to exactly this effect: "The whole secret of the teacher's force lies in the conviction that men are convertible. And they are. They want awakening."

My first real teaching job was at a place called the Woodstock Country School, a tiny boarding school in Vermont. The headmaster, Robin Leaver, who was an educational genius after his fashion, worked chiefly from one premise. "Every kid who enters this school," he'd often say, "has something that he can do at least half-well and probably a lot better; it's something he can take joy in; and it's something that he can use to make the world better. Your job as a teacher is to help each kid find that thing." We had marvelous students at Woodstock; some of them seemed to have a dozen or so gifts ready to unfold. But the ones who got the most tireless and affectionate attention from the teachers were the ones who seemed to have little or maybe nothing going for them. These were the kids that the world outside liked to call losers. In fact, their parents sometimes told us precisely that: "My kid's a loser. Good luck with her." Leaver, who had an affection for, and understanding of, sixteen-year-olds that I've never seen surpassed, would have to work hard to stop himself from detonating when he heard this sort of talk; usually he succeeded.

Every week, we got together in a faculty meeting and discussed each student. There were as many as seventy-five, so the meetings would sometimes go for three hours or more. The kids in the most trouble got the most time. I can still see Robin leaning over at us, vast smile, blond hair, movie-star good looks, nearly absurd for someone headmastering a school in outer nowhere, saying somewhat ironically (somewhat): "You call yourselves teachers and you can't find *anything* in the world that Michael Long is interested in? Nothing? Nothing?" Someone might observe that he'd seen Michael following Bruce around. Bruce was the farmer who grew crops on the school grounds and kept up the land. "Then what are we waiting for?" Leaver would say, "Let's put him to work with Bruce. He can study English and math next term."

Sometimes these shots in the dark worked, sometimes not. But what did have an effect was the students' developing awareness that the people who taught at the school would do anything, anything, to deliver them from wasted lives. Given that affirmation, the students were often inspired to start searching on their own.

Twenty-five years after Woodstock closed, at a reunion on what had been the school property, Robin and I talked about why the place had finally run aground. I said it was because to make ends meet we had to take too many kids who had too many problems. They were impossible. No, said Robin. Those kids would have come along. But some of them needed years and years at the school; we just didn't have enough time. In some empirical, practical sense, what I said may have been true. A few of the kids we were accepting at the end were borderline dangerous. But the one who spoke then in the true spirit of democratic education was surely not me.

Proust

PERHAPS THE LAST century's most persuasive theorist of positive influence is Marcel Proust. In luminous passages, he tells us how he developed as a reader, and then how, having himself become a writer, he hoped that he might affect others.

Proust observes: "The mediocre usually imagine that to let ourselves be guided by the books we admire robs our faculty of judgment of part of its independence. 'What can it matter to you what Ruskin feels: feel for yourself.' Such a view rests on a psychological error which will be discounted by all those who have accepted a spiritual discipline and feel thereby that their power of understanding and of feeling is infinitely enhanced, and their critical sense never paralyzed . . . There is no better way of coming to be aware of what one feels oneself than by trying to recreate in oneself what a master has felt. In this profound effort it is our own thought itself that we bring out into the light, together with his."

In a society that loves technique and training, but is wary of emotion not routinized by the newspaper or the sitcom, one must be willing to learn how to feel, then frequently to be reminded. This was the gift that Wordsworth gave to John Stuart Mill, who was, when he encountered the poet, dead in his life of feeling; a perpetual inner frost seemed to have taken hold. From this condition Wordsworth delivered him. Eliot tells us that one of the main functions of poetry is to give names, however complexly metaphorical the names might be, to emotions that have abided for a long time unspoken in the heart. To name feelings with poetic sensitivity, Eliot suggests, is to make them live yet more strongly. So, learning to feel with Ruskin, Proust learned to feel as himself.

The contemporary novelist Robert Stone describes his goal as a writer this way: "I want my reader to recognize what I've made and say, 'That's it. That's the way it is.'" No one describes this process of recognition, this benign literary influence, more gracefully than Proust, in the passages I cited in part at the beginning of this book: "But to return to my own case," Proust writes, "I thought more modestly of my book, and it would be inaccurate even to say that I thought of those who would read it as 'my' readers. For it seemed to me that they would not be 'my' readers but readers of their own selves, my book being merely a sort of magnifying glass like those which the optician at Combray used to offer his customers—it would be my book but with it I would furnish them with the means of reading what lay inside themselves. So that I would not ask them to praise me or to censure me, but simply to tell me whether 'it really is like that.' I should ask whether the words that they read within themselves are the same as those which I have written (though a discrepancy in this respect need not always be the consequence of an error on my part, since the explanation could also be that the reader had eyes for which my book was not a suitable instrument)."

Here Proust is remarkably sanguine about the possibility of the reader recognizing himself precisely in the mirror of the book's words. But often there is more to it than that. Recall Emerson: he that would bring home the wealth of the Indies must carry out the wealth of the Indies. Or, more dramatically,

Kierkegaard: he who would give birth to himself must know how to work. And so the visions of even the poets often need to be brought into line with our own aspirations and with the tempers of our times. Timeless in their uses as they may be, it can take skill to make them work here and now. As Proust in a more skeptical mood puts matters: "Reading is on the threshold of the spiritual life; it can introduce us to it: it does not constitute it."

Form and Feeling

WORDSWORTH SAID THAT he sought knowledge, but knowledge not purchased through the loss of power. Part of what makes literary education so important is that it offers something more than abstract knowing. It gives us wisdom that is replete with emotional force. The emphasis on form is what preserves art from the programmatic detachment that often informs more intellectualized ways of rendering experience.

There are many ways of thinking about form, from Kenneth Burke's Aristotelian view that form is the setting up and satisfying of expectations in the reader, to Kant's idea that form lifts the art object out of the push and toss of daily life and makes it a source for disinterested contemplation. But to me, form is best understood as the primary way that writers infuse their words with feeling. It provides the music of the work. Form is the sequence of notes that a sentence plays out, thus giving an emotional content to what could otherwise be a merely cognitive experience. And form is also the grander, symphonic structure of the work that lets us know in larger-scale terms what it would be like to live this vision—not moment to moment, as sentences do, but month to month, year to year. Where are the highs, where the despondencies?

The astounding comic buoyancy of a Dickens novel, its unflagging episodic invention, sprawling variety, and high-hearted tone, all contribute to a sense of what liberalism of Dickens's kind can be. For Dickens, liberalism isn't condescending, nor is it ever grudging; rather, it confers a vitality on the believer that makes him affirm life and hunger for more. And this is a function of the rambunctious form—sometimes it's an antiform, I suppose—of Dickens's major novels. Preeminently, form creates and reveals emotion.

The archetypal literary plot, the one adumbrated by Aristotle in *The Poetics*, can itself summon strong feelings. Many of us see ourselves in the protagonist who enters the world with strong desires, meets opposition and reversal, changes through struggle, and emerges richer—if in nothing else than in breadth of consciousness. For many, this pattern illuminates life. As Robert McKee, a thoughtful analyst of film, says, "Most human beings believe that life brings closed experiences of absolute, irreversible change; that their greatest sources of conflict are external to themselves; that they are the single and active protagonists of their own existence[s]; that their existence[s] operate through continuous time within a consistent, causally interconnected reality; and that inside this reality, events happen for explainable and meaningful reasons." An adroit deployment of conventional (or one might call it "archetypal") plot brings these convictions about life home to the reader with considerable impact—though the work need not articulate them overtly. Balzac's sense of what life is about—struggle, rivalry, triumph, bitter failure—is almost perfectly in tune with the values implicit in traditional novelistic plotting, and that is one of the reasons that his books read as satisfyingly as they do. In his best novels (I think of *White Noise* in particular) Don DeLillo departs from most of the assumptions that McKee lays out, not only in the way he renders character but also by shaping his books without readily apparent beginning, middle, and end. His cogent rebellion against novelistic form is, at least to me, as fruitful as Balzac's affirmation. It remains for the reader to say what form or antiform might put him into the best relation to his own experience. What is gained and what lost when you map your life according to the archetypal plot—or when, in DeLillo's fashion, you refuse that mapping?

It's quite possible that attempting to shape one's life, or interpret it, in conformity with traditional plot will lead to nothing but frustration. All of the relevant assumptions about character and cause and effect might lead to self-idealization and the failure that often attends it. But such a shaping could also offer intensity and focus. The individual who shares DeLillo's sense of the relatively haphazard way of the world may be better tuned to withstand life's vagaries, though for him, the dangers of fading toward entropy abide.

Literary beauty, to my mind, is the effective interfusion of feeling and thought. At the point of interfusion, though, there is no sentiment and there is no form—they have disappeared into each other, in the way that Apollo and Dionysus disappear into one another in Sophoclean drama, as Nietzsche understood it.

Form tells us how it feels to live the author's truth. "Know then thyself, presume not God to scan; / The proper study of mankind is Man." Pope's opening lines from the Second Epistle of "An Essay on Man," with their vigor, point, and strong but contained energy, make modesty—"presume not God to scan"—into a source of extreme self-assurance. Awareness of human limitation can quicken the spirit more, the lines suggest, than commitment to impious daring. In the music of the lines, in the form, is an entire attitude, a bearing. Form conveys to us how someone who spoke these lines feelingly might comport herself, how she'd move and talk and sit. Wordsworth's phrase "hearing oftentimes / The still, sad music of humanity" exudes a tentative melancholy evocative of the loneliness that suffuses a poem from which God has departed. The poem's view of the world is as much in its sonorous vowels as in its overt sense. Both Pope's lines and Wordsworth's are studies in perfect interfusion, both studies in literary beauty. "That's how it is. That's true." A reader could say as much of either of them.

Disciplines

The kind of reading that I have been describing here—the individual quest for what truth a work reveals—is fit for virtually all significant forms of creation. We can seek vital options in any number of places. They may be found for this or that individual in painting, in music, in sculpture, in the arts of furniture making or gardening. Thoreau felt he could derive a substantial wisdom by tending his bean field. He aspired to "know beans." He hoed for sustenance, as he tells us, but he also hoed in search of tropes, comparisons between what happened in the garden and what happened elsewhere in the world. In his bean field, Thoreau sought ways to turn language—and life—away from old stabilities.

Consider Proust, at the beginning of his career, writing to an editor to inquire if he might care for a piece of art criticism, one that would unfold the world view of the artist in something of the way, presumably, that Orwell unfolded Charles Dickens's: "I have just written a little study in the philosophy of art, if I may use that slightly pretentious phrase, in which I have tried to show how the great painters initiate us into a knowledge and love of the external world, how they are the ones 'by whom our eyes are opened,' opened that is, on the world. In this study, I use the work of Chardin as an example, and I try to show its influence on our life, the charm and wisdom with which it coats our most modest moments by initiating us into the life of still life. Do you think this sort of study would interest the readers of the *Revue Hebdomadaire*?"

The editor of the *Revue Hebdomadaire* thought not. But it would have interested me. For I think that in the works of all the consequential painters there is an answer to Schopenhauer's question "What is life?" That answer is difficult to coax forward, and few art critics have been able to do so. (Arnold Hauser comes most immediately to mind.) Such visions are easier to derive from words, from writings, in part because for most of us the prevailing medium, moment to moment, is verbal. We talk to ourselves. We talk to others. The circles that expand on the deep, or don't, are probably, for most of us, composed of words. Thus a critical part of making the non-verbal arts into the stuff of human expansion is verbal description. Criticism, acting in Proust's spirit, can turn the visions of the painters and composers into words, and so give us the chance to make better use of them. In humanistic criticism, there are few more difficult tasks than simply re-presenting a sculpture or a piece of music—describing the work and making it live.

I have chosen literature as a central source of vital words for a number of reasons. Since the Romantic period, literature has offered us a latent hypothesis. This is the view that there are simply too many sorts of human beings, too many idiosyncratic constitutions, for any one map of human nature, or any single guide to the good life, to be adaptable for us all. Such a realization, which coincides with the foundations of widespread democracy, as well as with the flourishing of novels, holds that there are multiple ways of apprehending experience, and multiple modes of internal organization, or disorder. Accordingly, there are many, many different ways to lead a satisfying, socially valuable life. This, as I've suggested, is what Milan Kundera is getting at when he calls the characters—and, by implication, the narrating voices—rendered in fiction "experimental selves." There are multiple ways to go, and confining theories of self, even those as penetrating as, say, Plato's and Kant's, cannot encompass the range of human difference.

The teacher begins the secular dialogue with faith by offering the hypothesis that there is no one human truth about the good life, but that there are many human truths, many viable paths. To set his students on them, he offers them multiple examples of what Arnold called the best that has been known and thought. This multiplying of possibilities—a condition enhanced by the rapid diffusion of culture around the globe—makes literature, which is inevitably the effusion of an individual mind, the most likely starting place, I would even say the center of humanistic education. As literary works are multiple, so are the number of potentially usable human visions of experience.

Beginning with this hypothesis, the teacher's task is often one of inspired impersonation. Against her students' Final Narratives, against their various faiths, she, with a combination of disinterest and passion, hurls alternatives. Impersonation: the teacher's objective is to offer an inspiring version of what is most vital in the author. She merges with the author, becomes the creator, and in doing so makes the past available to the uses of the present. The teacher listens to criticisms, perhaps engenders a few herself—but, always, ultimately, is the author's advocate, his attorney for explication and defense.

In this process it's important for the teacher to respect the possibility that however marvelous the books she puts before her students, some will in the end decide to stay as they are. They will wish, in Dr. Johnson's phrase, to repose upon the stability of truth—their own prior truth. Like Dr. Johnson, his contemporary Edmund Burke held certain conventional ways of thinking in the highest regard. Both men considered a nation's fund of common sense to be something like a slowly evolving epic poem, in which generation after generation deposited the wisdom it won through trial, success, error, and ensuing consideration.

In *Reflections on the Revolution in France*, Burke writes an homage to common wisdom, which he refers to under the name of prejudice, a word here devoid of its current racialist connotations. Teachers too eager to effect conversion should probably read Dr. Johnson and Edmund Burke regularly on the matter of conventional thinking at its best. Here is Burke addressing a sympathizer with revolutionary France: "We [in England] are generally men of untaught feelings; . . . instead of casting away all our old prejudices, we cherish them to a very considerable degree, and, to take more shame to ourselves, we cherish them because they are prejudices; and the longer they have lasted, and the more generally they have prevailed, the more we cherish them. We are afraid to put men to live and trade each on his own private stock of reason; because we suspect that this stock in each man is small, and that the individuals would do better to avail themselves of the general bank and capital of nations, and of ages. Many of our men of speculation, instead of exploding general prejudices, employ their sagacity to discover the latent wisdom which prevails in them. If they find what they seek, and they seldom fail, they think it more wise to continue the prejudice, with the reason involved, than to cast away the coat of prejudice, and to leave nothing but the naked reason; because prejudice, with its reason, has a motive to give action to that reason, and an affection which will give it permanence. Prejudice is of ready application in the emergency; it previously engages the mind in a steady course of wisdom and virtue, and does not leave the man hesitating in the moment of decision, skeptical, puzzled, and unresolved. Prejudice renders a man's virtue his habit; and not a series of unconnected acts. Through just prejudice, his duty becomes a part of his nature."

One might part company with Burke on the subject of how much power the individual mind can hope to possess—and I do—yet still listen respectfully to what he has to say about the "latent wisdom" that can inform conventional thinking. We need to be open to the possibility that our current students, who are less rebellious than any group I have encountered, may well know things that we do not.

History Now

THE METHOD OF teaching I affirm begins with the self and its own sense of who it is and what its destiny might be. But it is important not to end there. Humanistic education has to go beyond individual being. Emerson remarked once that there is no history, only biography. Admire Emerson as I do, here I think that he is trapped in outrageous error.

History has many uses for life. It begins as a branch of literature: Herodotus is determined to tell us about the great deeds of the Greeks who fought against the Persians, so that those deeds will not fade from human memory. He sets up his major figures, as Plutarch does his noble Greeks and Romans, as people worthy of emulation. In this respect, his work is in line with Homer and the epic poet's desire to preserve great deeds and great words for posterity. Herodotus offers the kind of exempla that literature, too, can give. From Plutarch to the present, Pericles to Rosa Parks, history is full of individuals who offer true inspiration.

But history doesn't only provide ideals. Its virtues are multiple. History too, one might say, is the noblest form of blackmail. Every leader of consequence knows that the eyes of the future will eventually fasten on him, and that he will pay with his reputation for even the best-hidden crimes. When Richard Nixon breaks through his manifold limits and opens up a dialogue with China, he's being responsive to history's noble blackmail.

In history, we also encounter large-scale narratives where we can find a place. Having made a commitment to, say, the teachings of the Savior, the future of socialism, or the progress of democracy, "an average unending procession," as Whitman described it, we want to locate the movement's origins. We want to see how the movement was born and what form its infancy and early growth took. And we want to join in the collective trajectory. By studying history we can attach ourselves to human efforts and human energies larger than ourselves and bring our personal force into the great wave of unfolding, collective hopes.

Literature, Aristotle tells us, is more philosophical than history; or, as Frye glosses him, philosophy presumes to tell us what must happen, history what has happened, and poetry what happens. There is the purportedly essential (philosophy), the contingent (history), and something in between (literature). But I would prefer to see in literature not so much a diagnosis of what happens but a prophecy of what can happen—a prophecy of how we can touch our version of that immortal freemasonry Keats describes. We are still trying to become the contemporaries of the great authors. Literature does many things. It puts us in contact with earthly hell, as we can best render it. But it also shows us the world we wish to live in, the place Blake and Frye think of when they use the word Golgonooza.

The cities that history unfolds are usually far different places. There what is most refractory about human experience reveals itself. Rome is built on slavery. Even exalted Athens burns with strife. Hegel refers to the slaughter bench of history; Marx talks about class struggle, but he might also have said class war, in which the descending classes are food for the upstarts. History, despite its glorious moments—despite the civil rights movement in America, despite the revolution that Jefferson and Washington led—is often a chronicle of misery. It shows where the best-laid plans tend to go.

History is frequently a cautionary antithesis to the hopes that literature ignites. For if *Lear* depicts horrors, one leaves the play nonetheless knowing that a human being wrote the play, a human being did *that*—and such achievement is a basis for hope. There is no such shaping force discernible behind history, despite the efforts of Hegelians of all stripes to reveal one. If literature and the arts can superbly render human freedom, history gives us the world of fate. And the student needs to measure every hope he has for self-creation, engendered by the poets and artists, against the realities of the recorded past. Not to be willing to engage this dialectic of power and limitation early on in life often condemns one to be the idealist in youth who becomes the disillusioned reactionary in old age. Without history to teach how hard it is, how ferociously fate can conspire against freedom, one is likely to be content with mere literary half-truths. Though the rise of democracy has injected a heretofore unimaginable hope into humanity's story, it still pays to consult history for a sense of how far we can fall and how fast.

In a liberal arts education, history is the necessary and profound rejoinder to the liberating arts—which is not to say that it cannot itself be a liberating art. But the literary comes first. Students need to be offered what hope they can accept, and to take it into a perilous future. Without a literary education, they may never find that hope. Fate, on the other hand, does not need to be sought and found. Fate will find you. History will find you. You can learn history from books, or life will teach it to you more intimately.

Always Historicize?

HISTORICIZING IS NOW the most influential intellectual fashion in the liberal arts. To qualify as a respectable scholar, one needs to put the work at hand into its historical context. That is, one must relegate it to the past. One must identify its analogues, its context, its conditions of engendering, the "social energies" that made it what it is. By no means should the real scholar see what the work can do in the present. That might open him up to criticism; it might make him look silly to actually profess something, rather than merely to affirm doubt and call it knowledge.

This is not to say that historical scholarship is without value. One needs to know the political context of Whitman's "Lilacs" elegy for President Lincoln; one needs to understand something of the Bible and something of Restoration politics to read Dryden's *Absalom and Achitophel*. But current scholars have gone far beyond that. To them, works of art are to be quarantined in the past, because living now we can't possibly understand them on their own terms. Good. We will understand them on what terms we can.

Scholars who historicize comprehensively, who deny the bearing of past greatness on the present, are persecuting the prophets, imprisoning their spirits. They are the descendants of Dostoyevsky's Inquisitor, who would protect the people from the dangerous word of the Savior by locking him away. I value few things as much as historical interpretations that allow us to read a past text in more nuanced ways. All honor to the bibliographers and the annotators. But to those who would clap the past away from the present—to paraphrase Blake at the close of *Milton*, they murder the Savior time on time.

True teachers of literature become teachers because their lives have been changed by reading. They want to offer others the same chance to be transformed. "What we have loved, / Others will love," says Wordsworth in *The Prelude*, "and we will teach them how." Literally the great poet is talking to his friend Coleridge, to whom the poem is written. But figuratively he speaks to all of us who have been changed by art and want to pay it forward, pass it along.

Why do teachers, especially at universities, turn against this hope, and teach that great writing is something we need to hold at arm's length? Why do they tell students to put the writing that matters at a historical distance, when students need to bring it closer to them, perhaps merge with it? To be entirely honest, I do not know. It may be that the weight of learning scholars must carry to be qualified to teach so stifles the imagination—so weighs it down—that it loses the power of sympathetic flight. This was what Nietzsche believed deep historical learning could do, and why he believed it was a danger as well as a potential virtue. There's a scene in Spenser where a questing knight is pinned down by the weight of his own armor, stuck to the ground and unable to fight. And that, perhaps, is the situation of our historicizers, pinned down by the bulk of their learning. As Nietzsche puts it, "The historical training of our critics prevents their having an influence in the true sense—an influence on life and action."

Or maybe institutional pressure for the conversion of imaginative power into academic knowledge is so strong that it forces the study of art to meet some high pseudo-scientific standards. Maybe we professors need to differentiate ourselves from grade school teachers (too feminine?) and show the investment bankers that we too are grown-ups, we too are mature? Does the need to be respected and respectable—the need to be beyond mockery—so infect university teachers that for it they sacrifice everything? Or are professors unwitting participants in the culture of cool, devoted to looking out at great art with the bemused, condescending detachment of the TV junkie? Have they taken up something not unlike the junkie's position, gazing down like slightly woozy gods on the passing show? Under the influence of dope (and its cultural equivalents), Ann Marlowe says, you can stem your anxieties. You can cultivate the illusion of having stopped time. But nothing Amazing will ever happen to you. (The changes that literature can bring on people are often just that, Amazing.)

Canons

ONCE YOU KNOW what purpose you want literature to fulfill—the purpose that all things that matter go to fulfill, as Emerson suggested: to inspire—then a span of questions that now bedevils the humanities becomes easier to answer. You can think much more clearly and to better effect about canon formation, about multiculturalism, about cultural studies, about academic research.

The question of canon formation, despite all its fancy baggage, is really a question about what to teach. What books shall we get young people to read? Right now this is a terribly vexed issue for a number of reasons. Traditionalists like to go around snorting about how the new cultural studies types want to replace Brontë novels with bodice rippers off the supermarket racks. But when you ask the traditionalists exactly what makes a Brontë novel more worth reading than a bodice ripper, they often can't come up with much. They talk about subtlety and sophistication and depth, and they take up a condescending pose, the pose smug upper-middle-class types have greeted the unwashed with for hundreds of years. And of course, the cultural studies gang loves this kind of reaction. They're fulfilling their historical function of shocking hell out of the bourgeoisie.

What the defenders of consequential writing need to do is to stand up and say that a Brontë novel can help you live better—can, to use the idiom of this book, better enhance your expanding circle of self than the bodice ripper can. Until the so-called humanists take this step, they're going to be easy prey to the prophets of ersatz novelty.

For myself, I would largely leave the question of what to teach up to individual teachers, who could offer those books that they think can change their students' lives for the better. Let them select the books that are full of vital options. Let them choose the works that they themselves have been transformed by and that they think, now, can have the greatest effect on students. Some of the best classes I had as a student came when the professor went back to a book he'd read when young and became that young man again, fired by Woolf, or Joyce, or Mann.

I think that canonical works, the ones you read as part of a major—the books of which there may be many or few, depending on the teachers' views at a given time—ought to be the testing and transforming books that have influenced people in exciting ways over a long period. Teachers must not be guided by what they find "interesting," or by what they sense might become the subject of a bracing essay for *PMLA,* but on what could inspire their students to change, or to solidify their own commitments. We all get socialized once by our parents and teachers, ministers and priests. Studying the humanities is about getting a second chance. It's not about being born again, but about growing up a second time, this time around as your own educator and guide, Virgil to yourself.

Scholarly discourse should be more and more about the educational, or self-developing, properties of great writing. An essay on Shakespeare and love ought not to unfold the "ideology" of Shakespearean love, but let us know what, if anything, the author thinks that Shakespeare has to teach us about Eros. Scholarly knowledge will still be at a premium, but its objective will be to bring forward the author's vision, to make explicit what is implicit, to show the way to successful teaching.

So absurdly removed from day-to-day life is professional

literary study that there is no major journal, on the order of *Raritan, Representations,* or *Critical Inquiry,* where teachers write to each other about ways they've found to teach this or that book. One has to look long and hard simply to find accounts of pedagogy. There are very, very few prominent scholars who have spent time writing about the actual dynamics of class exchange. In the waves of prose about the humanities that come out every year, students go virtually unmentioned. They are not quoted. They are not described. Anyone attending an academic conference or reading a professional journal for the first time would be forgiven for not knowing that what most of us spend most of our energies doing is teaching.

There is a sense among humanities professors that the field is drying up. All the major work has been done. Who wants to read yet another book on Alexander Pope? Well, I do, and students and common readers may as well, so long as the critic is willing to show what actual bearing Pope might have on the world we hold in common and on our individual lives. What human difference does he make? A brilliant book about Pope and the conduct of life could be of the highest value, and surely it is yet to be written. If what I am saying here is so, and literary criticism is not only a matter of interpretation, but a matter of reflecting on value, then the field is just opening up. The great bulk of meaningful work remains undone. And that, at least, might give some comfort to young people entering a field that must look utterly strip-mined.

I can't stress enough how despondent graduate students in the humanities often are at this point. They're some of the most admirable people to be found in their generation. With their prestigious undergraduate degrees, their splendid grades and board scores, they could go on to big-money careers in business and law. But they refuse. They want to study something that they're passionate about. Yet over time, almost all of them see that to thrive in the profession, they must make themselves marketable, and that often means betraying themselves. It means picking a subject that fits into the current conformity. It means spending years writing things that, on some deep level, they do not believe to be true. The exertion involved in having to get up every day, repair to one's word processor, and set to work defying one's nature in the interest of future employment, is not conducive to the psyche's health, or to the body's, either. These impressively gifted young men and women deserve better.

Their profession enjoins them to seek not what is true and humanly transforming but what is "interesting." That is, they seek out areas for research that are untouched, often untouched for very good reason. So the assistant professor begins a deep study of now unread and barely readable nineteenth-century domestic novels or boys' adventure books. Then he begins to teach those books, the better to get the monograph done, and in doing so becomes a waster of students' most valuable time and accordingly of students' lives. If a professor truly believes that nineteenth-century domestic fiction can expand the reader, make him more than he was, that is wonderful. I respect the daring. The independence of mind is to be admired. But to teach without the conviction that the book at hand might become someone's secular Bible is to betray the heart of the humanities.

To some, it may seem that literary study is at its end. But I believe we may be at the inception. We can begin to come to terms with Arnold's view that in the absence of faith in transcendental religion, poetry may have to do. We can begin learning to talk about poetry in order to render it as the secular scripture that it needs to be.

Do students, in order to be changed, need to read books that touch on their own experience, and in particular their own identity? Sometimes. If you are to adapt the world of a book to your own, to be influenced by it, it's probably helpful for the book to intersect with your past experience. So occasionally it will only be sensible for the young black man to start with Malcolm X, for the young black woman to pick up Zora Neale Hurston.

But identification also moves across the boundaries of race, class, and gender. I, growing up in the white working class, found no book more fascinating when I was seventeen than *The Autobiography of Malcolm X.* From Malcolm I learned a good deal about race relations in America; I learned about the forms of racism endemic to the South, but also, more shockingly, to the North, where I was growing up. (We were virtuous, we white northerners, especially compared with the mad Confederates we saw on TV hurling rocks in Selma—or so I imagined before I read Malcolm X.) But I acquired other things from that book as well. Malcolm X learned to read and write well in prison, relatively late in life. In page after rhapsodic page, he describes the joys of reading, the pleasures of expression, the lure of knowledge. Malcolm was persuaded, and persuaded me, that you could use the powers you acquired from books to live better yourself and to do something for the people around you. In terms of literal identity, Malcolm X and I had virtually nothing in common, but reading his book shaped me in ways that continue to matter thirty-five years after the first encounter.

So by all means, give the young black student who's barely heard of Malcolm a copy of the *Autobiography.* But we shouldn't assume that an African American is inevitably going to be more responsive to Malcolm than to Marcel Proust. If, on getting to college, I had encountered professors convinced that I needed to read James T. Farrell, Mike Gold, or some other designated "proletarian writers," I would have rebelled instantly. At the same time I was glad to read Farrell, among many others, and found in him something of an ally. One's literal identity—the product of race, class, gender, and socialization—is not the sole, and very often not even the central, ground for literary identification.

Multiculturalism

KNOW THE OTHER, says the multiculturalist. I agree. A segment of the humanities curriculum *should* be devoted to studying the literature and arts of cultures that are so resolutely different from the West's that what we confront is less likely to be live options than it is bracingly different modes of being. It is a good thing to know and respect difference, if it is worthy of respect, and to understand other cultures in their own terms.

Such knowledge may impede cruelty and exploitation, granted. But shall we know the other without knowing ourselves? If we learn only of difference, without taking the time to find, or begin to compound, the inner being, we risk being walking voids, readily taken up by, say, commercial interests, ever ready to use our college-won knowledge of others for the purposes of exploiting them. Where the inner void was, the unbearable lightness was, there the corporation may well drive its roots. Knowledge of the other without a corresponding self-knowledge is a supremely dangerous acquisition.

There may be no better training for the global economy than multiculturalism. Students who are immersed in this curriculum will find that they are able to pose as "citizens of the world,"

moving among many sorts of people. But in whose interest?
Who benefits? Will the world? Writing on the rise of multicultural education, David Rieff
asks a sharp question: "Are the multi-culturalists truly unaware
of how closely their treasured catchphrases—'cultural diversity,'
'difference,' the need to 'do away with boundaries'—resemble
the stock phrases of the modern corporation: 'product diversi-
fication,' 'the global marketplace,' and 'the boundary-less company'?" Later in his essay, Rieff observes: "The more one reads
in academic multi-culturalist journals and in business publications, and the more one contrasts the speeches of CEOs and the
speeches of noted multiculturalist academics, the more one is
struck by the similarities in the way they view the world . . . Both
CEOs and Ph.D.'s insist more and more that it is no longer
possible to speak in terms of the United States as some fixed,
sovereign entity. The world has moved on; capital and labor are
mobile; and with each passing year national borders, not to
speak of national identities, become less relevant either to
consciousness or to commerce."

Martha Nussbaum, one of the few thinkers now who is
willing to suggest that literature and art matter because they
can help people to live better than they do, argues that
becoming a citizen of the world is the objective of liberal arts
education. This goal she attributes to the Greeks. But what
Socrates, primary among Greek thinkers, taught first is to
know yourself. And when you do, through literature and
history, you will begin to see whether being a citizen of the
world is the right thing for you to aspire to be at this point in
time. Perhaps the goal of world citizenship is too abstract.
Maybe we need to be more pragmatic. How, precisely, does
one wish to connect to the world at large? Maybe the best
relation to the existing world, if global capitalism is the

prevailing game, will be pure opposition, anti-world-citizenship as it were.

But multiculturalism, well understood, remains one of the joys of current humanistic study. The scholarly work of bringing together East and West, for instance, is of the greatest consequence. The religious thought and the medical knowledge of the East have a great deal to teach us in our present state. Never have we had a chance to learn so much from the study of others, including a humane, but not a blindly comprehensive, tolerance. And some texts that initially seem embodiments of pure difference will turn out to be exactly the ones that future students respond to with a shock of recognition. The young upper-middle-class woman from Ohio may turn away from Virginia Woolf's *To the Lighthouse*, a book she's supposed to adore, and find that Chinua Achebe sees the world almost precisely as it is. Once we've opened up the possibility of direct literary connection—connection with great authors in the search for truth—all sorts of marvelous and unexpected meetings of mind become possible.

Pop

THE SPIRIT OF education I affirm is well expressed by Harold Bloom: "We all of us go home each evening, and at some moment in time, with whatever degree of overt consciousness, we go back over all the signs that the day presented to us. In those signs, we seek only what can aid the continuity of our own discourse, the survival of those ongoing qualities that will give what is vital in us even more life. This seeking is the Vichian and Emersonian making of signification into meaning, by the single test of aiding our survival." This is what we do, or ought to do, with books—turn their signification into meaning, and so into possibility, in the hopes that so doing will better our lot.

The test of a book lies in its power to map or transform a life. The question we would ultimately ask of any work of art is this: Can you live it? If you cannot, it may still command considerable interest. The work may charm, it may divert. It may teach us something about the larger world; it may refine a point. But if it cannot help some of us to imagine a life, or unfold one already latent within, then it is not major work, and probably not worth the time of students who, at this period in their lives, are looking to respond to consequential and very pressing questions. They are on the verge of choosing careers, of marrying, of entering the public world. They are in dire need of maps, or of challenges to their existing cartography. Perhaps most of all, they seek ways to unfold their promise, to achieve the highest form of being they can. Works of art matter to the degree that they can help people do this. Books should be called major and become canonical when over time they provide existing individuals with live options that will help them change for the better. A democratic humanism can have no other standard for greatness.

The most beautiful statement of this ideal of literary education that I know of is Oscar Wilde's and comes from "The Soul of Man Under Socialism": "So he who would lead a Christ-like life is he who is perfectly and absolutely himself. He may be a great poet, or a great man of science; or a young student at a University, or one who watches sheep upon a moor; or a maker of dramas, like Shakespeare, or a thinker about God, like Spinoza; or a child who plays in a garden, or a fisherman who throws his nets into the sea. It does not matter what he is, as long as he realizes the perfection of the soul that is within him. All imitation in morals and in life is wrong. Through the streets of Jerusalem at the present day crawls one who is mad and carries a wooden cross on his shoulders. He is a symbol of the lives that are marred by imitation. Father Damien was Christ-like when he went out to live with the lepers, because in such service he realized fully what was best in him. But he was not more Christ-like than Wagner, when he realized his soul in music; or than Shelley, when he realized his soul in song. There is no one type for man. There are as many perfections as there are imperfect men." Such perfections are the aim of literary education, and if perfection is rarely the actual result, the process is no less noble for that.

Popular culture, which is more and more taught at universities, usually cannot offer such prospects. The objective of a good deal of rock music and film is to convey the pleasing illusion that people can live in the way that the singers and the actors do when they're on. Occasionally, I suppose, a performer comes through. Keith Richards seems to be, in life, the Keith he evokes when he's onstage. Most people probably don't have the guts or the constitution. When Terry Southern came to interview Richards, he laid three Quaaludes on him as a gift. Keith swallowed them all, took a slug of bourbon, and woke up two days later. No interview for Terry. But I'm not sure that this moment, taken as representative, can point to a plausible life for much of anyone except Richards himself.

Yet what David Denby says about movie love—and by extension the love of popular culture overall—still strikes me as true: "Movie love puts people in touch with their own instincts and pleasures. Movies can lead to self-reconciliation, and that is one reason they have inspired an almost unlimited affection." Putting people in touch with their instincts and pleasures: movies and many other popular forms tap into the fantasy life, and insofar as desire is being drowned by the gray waves of the reality principle, we need it to be restored. (Not to be able to fantasize at all is probably even less healthy than fantasizing all the time.) A little bit of tolerant thinking about the sorts of erotic and adventurous fantasies that we're drawn to can tell us a good deal about what's not present in our own lives. The message may be hyperbolical; fantasy is an exaggerated genre. But perhaps we need such exaggeration to be awakened from the spell of the day-to-day. Fantasy can inspire us to search for ways to satisfy hungers we didn't know we had.

By far the best inquiry into pop culture I know of along these lines is Simon Frith's essay on the Stones' *Beggar's Banquet*. "I've always lived a decent, sober, careful life," says Frith, disarmingly enough, and then he goes on to describe what it means to him to be drawn to the woozy, reckless life the Stones purvey. By the end of the piece, Frith can say that "*Beggar's Banquet*, so intense in its pursuit of pleasure, lays bare the weight borne by our notions of love and sex, the secret melancholy of life in the consumer collective. These are as much effects of current capitalism as dole queues and boring jobs and material squalor[,] and the Stones' pleasure perspective gives us a new sense of them . . . In other words, the function of the Stones' rock and roll dedication . . . is not self-indulgence or escape but defiance. *Beggar's Banquet* celebrates the reality of capitalist pleasure and denies its illusions. No expectations, a lot of laughs—the Stones' strength derives from their prodigality, from their denial of consequence." That said, the "decent, sober, careful" author has probably got to think about some riskier, more pleasure-prone ways to live.

Once we have made contact with fantasy, we need a new, larger self-synthesis that pays heed to refractory desires. Self-knowledge means knowing what we want, even if those wants are embarrassingly grandiose, or socially despised. But fantasies cannot generally be a direct blueprint for life, the way that the work of Henry James, say, can conceivably be.

Denby's article on film is related to Freud's radically under-valued essay "Creative Writers and Daydreaming." Here Freud, always competing with literature, wants to associate it with the id, giving psychoanalysis pride of place as the best way to develop the sane ego. Freud says that creative writing is simply a form of wish-fulfillment. In fiction and poetry of every sort, we find pleasurable fantasies to enjoy. What keeps us from seeing literary texts—not some, but all—as the fantasies that they are is form. Form, to Freud, is a distancing device. It offers the ego something to occupy itself, a kind of fore-pleasure, preliminary to the id's immersing itself in wish-fulfillment. In other words, form plays the role for lit-erature, and presumably the other arts, that the dream work—the mechanisms by which the desire at the center of the dream undergoes distortion—plays in dreams.

Surely, though, it's not only form that makes John Milton definingly different from the latest pop best-seller. One can still live out of Milton's *Paradise Lost*, a poem that has a word, however harsh, to say about virtually every subject that matters. What ought to make a work survive is that it can be lived, can function, as Milton very much wished his poem to do, as a Bible of sorts. *Paradise Lost* was Freud's favorite poem, and, like all of the major works Freud pondered, from *Oedipus Rex* to *Lear*, it is a basis for psychoanalysis. Those works are far too tough-minded to be written off as wish-fulfillments, just as psycho-analysis is far too sophisticated, at its best, to boil down to the worship of one more spectral figure of authority, Sigmund Freud. Pop culture is by and large where wishes thrive, and knowing as much reveals pop culture's great value, as well as its limits.

Of course pop culture can be an area for productive disagreement. Given the work at hand, different people will respond differently to the question of whether you can live it out. Some will say yes to Bob Dylan (as I would, with reservations), yes to Muddy Waters and the blues tradition he works in, yes to Robert Altman or Stanley Kubrick. But you'll find far fewer people, I think, who'll be able to say an unequivocal yes to the Rolling Stones or to Britney Spears. That doesn't mean that the Rolling Stones and, who knows, maybe even Britney, are without their value (fantasy matters). But teaching such work to people who're looking for answers to primary questions may not be the best way to use their time.

Not long ago, I met a student who told me an illuminating story. The student, now in college, had a high school English teacher whom he'd greatly admired, and that teacher admired Faulkner above all writers. For his part, the student admired Stephen King. He read everything King wrote; he loved his work. The teacher detested King. Why? Because, the teacher said, unlike Faulkner, King did not write "works of universal human significance."

The student walked away angry and unsatisfied, and I don't blame him. How does this teacher know what is "universal" and what is not? How does he know what something called the "human" might be? Only God—if he exists—knows what "universal human significance" is.

What the teacher might have said is something like this: "King is an entertainment. King is a diversion. But when you try to take him as a guide to life, he won't work. The circles he draws on the deep are weak and irresolute. And this is so in part because King, for all his supposedly shocking scare tactics, is a sentimental writer. In his universe, the children (or at least the pack of nice kids, the ones the bullies prey on) are good, right, just, and true. (In Wordsworth, the child is a much more complex being, appealing but not without his dangerous limits.) When King's kids see It—whether It is a spaceship, a slasher-clown from the deep past, or a ravenous vampire—It is truly there. Just about all adults who are not in some manner child-like are corrupt, depraved, lying, and self-seeking. This can be a pleasant fantasy for young people and childish adults. Facile Rousseauianism has its temporary pleasures. But bring this way of seeing the world out into experience and you'll pretty quickly pay for it. Your relation to large quadrants of experience, in particular those where you have to encounter adult authority, will likely be paranoid and fated to fail. On the other hand, Faulkner's tragic humanism is tough; it could stand the test of time. There's a lot to be learned from Dilsey, the black woman in *The Sound and the Fury*, who above all things endures. But that's not because she illuminates some 'universal human significance,' but because she does her work and lives righteously in the world."

When we teachers stop giving self-inflating answers to our students, and become clearly articulate about what the humanities can and can't offer—they may help you live better; they won't help you be a god—we'll be on our way to justifying our work to the public and attracting the students who most need us. Students now live in a bubbling chaos of popular culture. They need a way to navigate it. They need to know what's worth taking seriously, and what's a noisy diversion. We in the humanities can help them make this distinction. The mark of an educated person should be the ability to see the differences between entertainment and more nurturing, vital stuff. We need to help the public see how to make use of what great books offer. When people can do as much, they'll be able to take plenty of harmless pleasure in pop.

Many humanities teachers feel that they are fighting for a lost cause. They believe that the proliferation of electronic media will eventually make them obsolete. They see the time their students spend with TV and movies and on the Internet, and feel that what they have to offer—words, mere words—must look shabby by comparison.

Not so. When human beings try to come to terms with who they are and describe who they hope to be, the most effective medium is words. Through words we represent ourselves to ourselves; we fix our awareness of who and what we are. Then we can step back and gain distance on what we've said. With perspective comes the possibility for change. People write about their lives in their journals; talk things over with friends; talk, at day's end, to themselves about what has come to pass. And then they can brood on what they've said, privately or with another. From that brooding comes the chance for new beginnings. In this process, words allow for precision and nuance that images and music generally don't permit.

Our culture changes at an astounding velocity, so we must change or pay a price for remaining the same. Accordingly, the powers of self-rendering and self-revision are centrally important. These processes occur best in language. Surely there is something to be learned from the analysis of popular culture. But we as teachers can do better. We can strike to the central issues that confront students and the public at large, rather than relegating ourselves to the edges. People who have taught themselves how to live—what to be, what to do—from reading great works will not be overly susceptible to the culture indus-

try's latest wares. They'll be able to sample them, or turn
completely away—they'll have better things on their minds.

Democracy and Faith

THIS BOOK TOOK off from some lines of William Carlos
Williams's: The new is in despised poems, he said, and men die
every day for lack of what is found there. What is found there
that prevents death, or death-in-life, is meaning—more precisely, meaning that can do something like what religious
conviction can.

"The future of poetry is immense," Matthew Arnold wrote,
"because in poetry, where it is worthy of its high destinies, our
race, as time goes on, will find an ever surer and surer stay. There
is not a creed which is not shaken, not an accredited dogma
which is not shown to be questionable, not a received tradition
which does not threaten to dissolve. Our religion has materi-
alized itself in the fact, in the supposed fact; it has attached its
emotion to the fact, and now the fact is failing it. But for poetry
the idea is everything. . . ."

Arnold tells us that if religious faith wanes in the world—or in
a given individual—then the next likely source of meaning will
be literature. The literature we have come to value, most
especially the novel, is by and large antitranscendental. It does
not offer a vision of the world under a deity's guidance. It
suggests, though often it doesn't assert, that we humans have to
make our own way without the strains and the comforts of faith.

The teaching of literature I believe in does not argue that
always and for everyone, a secular, imaginative vision has to
replace faith. My sort of teaching assumes that a most pressing
spiritual and intellectual task of the moment is to create a

dialogue between religious and secular visions of the world. Many of my students leave class with their religious convictions deepened and ramified. They're more ardent, more thoughtful believers than when they arrived. The aim is not conversion. The aim is encounter between the transcendental and the worldly. The objective is to help students place their ultimate narratives in the foreground and open themselves up to influence.

Religious faith in America now seems very strong. Somehow, in a culture that has disenchanted everything, a culture where cool prevails, religion has remained relatively intact. But I continue to feel that, as Freud expressed it in his 1927 book *The Future of an Illusion*, the promise for a large-scale turn away from religion is near at hand. There is simply too little evidence—at least by the relatively scientific standards that we now rely on in other areas of inquiry—that the miraculous tales that come to us in the Scriptures are true. Religion has attached itself to the fact, as Arnold says, "and now the fact is failing it." Efforts to prove God's existence materially and logically have never been fully satisfying. Just so, to believe intuitively in an all-loving, merciful, and omnipotent God is difficult for many of us after a century of closely documented horrors. Why didn't this Omnipotence intervene? Why didn't he prevent the horrible deaths of children and of relatively innocent women and men?

It may well be a matter of time, as Freud suggested, before lack of hard evidence combines with the absence of experiential proof to turn great masses of people against religion. But there is also the fact that many of the people in America now who claim to be religious have what is at best a tenuous purchase on faith. Their religions, often self-concocted, are Religion Lite, narcissistic investments in guardian angels and smilingly bland deities. There are few resources in such faiths to deal with tragedy and horror. When those things come to pass, how long will our current fragile faiths—think of my student's Catherinism—actually last? And if religion fails, what will there be to replace it? How will we give a meaning and shape to life? How will we tell ourselves stories, collective and individual, about our time here that can make life worth living?

Freud, for his part, commends a bleak stoicism as a replacement for faith. We need to face the fact that this life is full of undeserved, unredeemable suffering. We need to alleviate as much of that suffering as we can, not for any transcendental reason, but because it is in our interest to live in societies that do all they can to ease pain. Beyond that there is simple endurance. In his marvelous elegy, Auden commends Freud for achieving a fully compassionate regard for humanity: "Every day they die / Among us, those who were doing us some good, / And knew it was never enough but / Hoped to improve a little by living. / Such was this doctor."

Nietzsche, another major source for these thoughts on teaching and learning, felt the absence of God far more dramatically than Freud did. He saw God's death—by which he meant, among other things, the passing away of God's perceived presence from day-to-day life—as a traumatic event in human history, one whose full impact was not yet clear to most of humanity. It has still perhaps not reached us. The presence of God compelled human beings to quest for an ideal. They had to strive for something to win God's blessing—even if what they strove for was often not at all congenial to Nietzsche. Nietzsche feared that with the passing of God even that striving would stop. No one would think it worth his while to try to overcome himself. People would live happily with their own limitations.

To move from a world peopled by Homeric heroes striving for the first place, to a world in which the best men and women struggled to please God by abasing themselves was cause for lament. But worse was life in which humanity had lost all interest in ideals. This was the world epitomized by "the Last Man." This creature who hops and blinks on the earth's crust, small and self-seeking, lives with the most pitiable credo: "One still works, for work is a form of entertainment. But one is careful lest the entertainment be too harrowing. One no longer becomes poor or rich: both require too much exertion. Who still wants to rule? Who obey? Both require too much exertion." The Last Man has his "little poison now and then: that makes for agreeable dreams"; he is cautious, self-absorbed, noncommittal. "We have invented happiness," the Last Men say, and then they blink.

What happens now and in the future if our most intelligent students never learn to strive to overcome what they are? What if aspirations to genius, and to contact with genius through Keats's immortal free-masonry, become silly, outmoded ideas? What you're likely to get are more and more two-dimensional men and women. These will be people who live for easy pleasure, for comfort and prosperity and the satisfactions of cool, who think of money first, then second, and third; who hug the status quo; people who believe in God as a sort of insurance policy (cover your bets); people who are never surprised. They will be people so pleased with themselves (when they're not in despair at the general pointlessness of their lives) that they cannot imagine that humanity could do better. They'll think it their highest duty to have themselves cloned as often as possible. They'll claim to be happy and they'll live a long time.

Against the coming of the Last Man, Nietzsche had little to

recommend. He said that we might place ourselves thoroughly on the side of fate, and affirm the eternal recurrence of the same thing, no matter how horrible events might be. Our objective would be to turn the past ("Thus it was") into a function of our own desire ("Thus I willed it") and so come to love our fate. Our goal would be to take any event, no matter how horrible, and use it in our project of self-creation. We might use such events as a motive for growth or as raw material for works of art that would enlarge the mind. "What does not kill me," Nietzsche said in a self-vaunting moment, "makes me stronger."

But who could really affirm the eternal recurrence of everything? Who would have the demonic strength to wish for the Holocaust to happen again? Who could find possibilities for human expansion in that? And if you cannot affirm all events, including the most horrible, then surely the doctrine of the eternal recurrence dwindles in its power.

Neither Freud nor Nietzsche has Arnold's faith in the capacity of literature to create meanings that might, at the least, make life bearable. To Freud, literature was illusion, mere wish-fulfillment. To Nietzsche, the lure of large-scale philosophical answers, answers that might be for everyone, or for everyone who mattered, such as the commitment to eternal recurrence, pushed the prospect of literary response aside.

Literary response is individual, particular: to put trust in literature affirms the antiphilosophic view that there are as many ways of living well as there are individuals disposed to do so. Nietzsche and Freud are aristocrats by temperament. The turn to literature for multiple truths is a democratic turn. The conviction that each of us has a particular genius to unfold is a democratic conviction.

Some will object to an open-ended vision of education in which we pursue our own visions, our own truths. People can become distressed when they imagine a world in which all of us, inspired by poets and other artists, create our lives, with only the inhibitions of community welfare and of our perceived failures to rein us in. They fear chaos, they say. They fear disorder. But perhaps what they fear, most truly, is genuine democracy.

And there is a sense in which they are quite right to be wary. For understood in its full implications, democracy is a gamble. People educated to enjoy the freedom of the poets may not always make the right choices, and surely they will not always make choices that we ourselves would approve. Jean Paul Sartre says that no great work of literature could ever be anti-Semitic. It's pretty to think so. Consider Christopher Marlowe's *Jew of Malta* or Shakespeare's *Merchant of Venice*. Both are great imaginative achievements; both, whatever ingenuity a director may deploy to stage them, madly anti-Semitic at their cores. The fact is that literature can do us harm. It's a gamble to put our faith in it. It's a gamble to think of leaving religion behind.

Democratic humanism is a risk. We are betting that people will prefer life to death, creation to destruction, freedom to servitude. They have not always shown a will to do so.

All through time the consensus has been that people cannot rule themselves. In the great mass, they're depraved. They need to be controlled. The people at the top of the heap know best. But in America, we've decided to defy that long-standing wisdom. We've taken many steps toward the goal of full franchise for all, but there's further to go. We need to begin educating people now with full respect for their powers of determination. We need to give them the resources of the best that has been known and thought, and then stand back and let them make the decisions that matter.

The more chance that people have fully and freely to unfold themselves, the more chance, ultimately, that they'll find their own happiness, and the more chance that they will enlarge the scope of the possible for others. In every life-affirming human mutation, however apparently odd, there lies the chance that something new and wonderful will arise that will act as a light to future generations. If America leads and inspires the world in the years to come, it will not be because we have the most potent armies, or create the most alluring entertainments, or manufacture the best products, or even create the most wealth. It will be because here more than anywhere, people are free to pursue their own hopes of becoming better than they are in a human sense—wiser, more vital, kinder, sadder, more thoughtful, more worth the admiration of their children. And it will be because they are free to become who they aspire to be after their own peculiar fashions. They'll feel a just pride in themselves and they'll feel a tough and enduring pride in a country that trusted them enough to let them flourish. Democracy wagers that when you put human beings together and give them every opportunity to express and develop themselves, then their virtues will exceed their faults, if only by so much. To be part of that experiment, and to contribute to its success, that is something that a man or woman, however humble, can take a vast and honest pride in.

Democracy, and the democratic humanism that can make it unfold—these are my religion. These are the sources of my faith and hope. For the promises of democratic humanism are without bound. Imagine a nation, or world, where people have fuller self-knowledge, fuller self-determination, where self-making is a primary objective not just in the material sphere but in the circles of the mind and heart. ("It tends outward," that heart, "to immense and innumerable expansions.") We humanities teachers can help create such a world, a world of rich, inter-animating individuality, in tandem with flourishing community. A renewed democratic humanism can take us there. We should begin, now, to heed that humanism's highest promise.

Acknowledgments

THIS IS A book that was written in nearly ideal circumstances, and for that I have many to thank. Thanks first to my students at the University of Virginia and to my colleagues in the English Department there. They contributed to making this work something like a pleasure.

Lewis Lapham of *Harper's Magazine* helped to get the book off the ground with an idea about an essay on the liberal arts. Many thanks to him. To develop early thoughts into book form, I spent a term in residence at the Virginia Foundation for the Humanities, where I enjoyed the hospitality of Roberta Culbertson, Robert Vaughan, and Andrew Wyndham. A pair of summer grants from the University of Virginia also sped me on my way.

For the first draft of this book, I couldn't have had better readers. I thank Richard Rorty, for astute commentary and suggestions on philosophical matters. Thanks, too, to David Lenson; a sentence of his on the matter of prose and jalapeño peppers was worth pages. Thanks to Michael Pollan, not only for his editorial suggestions, which were, as always, superb, but for the unpriceable gift of thirty years of friendship. With this book, as with all my books, he was with me from start to finish.

From this generous trinity, the book traveled to Chris Calhoun, agent and sage, who did me no end of good turns, as he always has. The day I met Chris was one of my luckiest. Gillian Blake, brilliant and humane editor, responded right away to this project and lighted its way to completion.

Thanks too to Douglas Myers, known elsewhere as Franklin

Lears, teacher and friend, whose conversation now and example long ago helped shape these thoughts. For suggestions and good will, thanks to Megan Marshall, Ed Ayers, Allan Megill, Steve Cushman, Michael Levenson, Jahan Ramazani, Jessica Feldman, Karen Chase, Gordon Braden, Paul Cantor, Jackson Lears, and Adam Phillips. Chip Tucker responded to the manuscript with careful suggestions and weighty challenges: many thanks to him. Thanks too to my Sunday basketball brethren, and to my esteemed teachers at 206.

I'm grateful to the audiences who heard these thoughts out: corroborated, revised, and challenged them. They were at the University of Virginia (particular thanks to Marva Barnett and the Teaching Resource Center), James Madison University, Hendrix College, the University of Hartford, New College, Lehigh University, Keene State College, the University of Richmond, Williams College, Smith College, Florida Atlantic University, Duke University, Wake Forest University, and Haverford College.

My wife, Liz, and my sons, Willie and Matthew, gave me endless love and understanding and (it came mostly from Willie, but not only) some loud, loud, sweet rock and roll.

Mark Edmundson is NEH/Daniels Family Distinguished Teaching Professor at the University of Virginia. A prizewinning scholar, he has published a number of works of literary and cultural criticism, including *Literature Against Philosophy, Plato to Derrida*, as well as a memoir, *Teacher: The One Who Made the Difference*. He has also written for such publications as the *New Republic*, the *New York Times Magazine*, the *Nation*, and *Harper's*, where he is a contributing editor.

A NOTE ON THE TYPE

The text of this book is set in Linotype Sabon, named after the type founder Jacques Sabon. It was designed by Jan Tschichold and jointly developed by Linotype, Monotype, and Stempel, in response to a need for a typeface to be available in identical form for mechanical hot metal composition and hand composition using foundry type.

Tschichold based his design for Sabon roman on a font engraved by Garamond, and Sabon italic on a font by Granjon. It was first used in 1966 and has proved an enduring modern classic.